The M Hilarious

After-Dinner Jokes & Stories

Compiled by Gerry Howe

Published by
PPGS
LONDON

First published in Great Britain by
PPGS
PO Box 42
Princes Risborough
Bucks.
HP27 0XH

©PPGS/KCS 2003

ISBN 0-9540822-1-4

Printed in The United Kingdom
by Cox & Wyman Ltd, Reading

Dedication

Dedicated to my many friends around the world, who constantly call, write and overflow my email inbox with mirth and merriment.

Among these, special mentions must go to
Derek Searle, John Wilson, Peter Hornby,
Bob Cripps, Nick Potts, Michael Briggs, Malcolm Corby,
Carol Coleman, Cathy Ayling, Pam Leaper, Stewart & Mandy
David Goold, Dave Levin, Alan Bland, Peter Halls,
Richard Mallows and David Huskinson
for their imagination, sense of humour and consistent supply!

Also my warmest thanks go to the team that helped make this publication possible
Derek, John, & Peter

Always remember to keep it in perspective.........
Don't take life too seriously...
You won't get out alive!

FIRE DRILL

A Jamaican fireman came home from work one day and said to his wife :
"Y'know sumpin, we have de wonderful new system at de fire station.

Bell 1 rings - we put on our jackets.
Bell 2 rings - we slide down de pole.
Bell 3 rings - we jump on de ingine and we's a ready to go.

From now on, when I say....
'Bell one' I want you to strip naked.

When I say Bell two', you jump on de bed.

When I says 'Bell tree, we's gonna make love all tru' de night."

The next night he came home and shouted:
'Bell One' and she stripped naked.
'Bell Two' and she jumped on the bed.
'Bell Tree', and they started to make love.

After a few minutes the wife yelled out "Bell Four".
" What de hell is 'Bell Four'?"

She replied: "Roll out more hose, man, you ain't nowhere near de fire."

THE CLASSIC BANK ROBBERY!

Excerpt from an article which appeared in the Dublin Times about a bank robbery on March 2.

Once inside the bank shortly after midnight, their efforts at disabling the security system got underway immediately.

The robbers, who expected to find one or two large safes filled with cash & valuables, were surprised to see hundreds of smaller safes throughout the bank.

The robbers cracked the first safe's combination, and inside they found only a small bowl of vanilla pudding. As recorded on the bank's audiotape system, one robber said, "At least we'll have a bit to eat."

The robbers opened up a second safe, and it also contained nothing but vanilla pudding. The process continued until all safes were opened.

They did not find one-pound sterling, a diamond, or an ounce of gold.

Instead, all the safes contained covered bowls of pudding.

Disappointed, the robbers made a quiet exit, each leaving with nothing more than a queasy, uncomfortably full stomach.

The following day the newspaper headline read

IRELAND'S LARGEST SPERM BANK ROBBED EARLY THIS MORNING!

So I was having dinner with
Gary Kasporov (world chess champion)
and there was a check tablecloth.

It took him two hours to pass me the salt

~~~~~~~~~~~~~~~~~~~~~~~~~~~~~~~~~~~~~~

Thought For The Day:

Don't sweat the petty things
And don't pet the sweaty things.

Hi Honey, I'm out Shopping!

Several men are in the locker room of a golf club. A cell phone on a bench rings and a man engages the hands free speaker-function and begins to talk.

MAN: "Hello"

WOMAN: "Honey, it's me. Are you at the club?"

MAN: "Yes"

WOMAN: "I am at the mall now and found this beautiful leather coat. It's only $1,000. Is it OK if I buy it?"

MAN: "Sure, ...go ahead if you like it that much."

WOMAN: "I also stopped by the Mercedes dealership and saw the new 2003 models. I saw one I really liked."

MAN: "How much?"

WOMAN: "$60,000"

MAN: "OK, but for that price I want it with all the options."

WOMAN: "Great! Oh, and one more thing....the house we wanted last year is back on the market. They're asking $950,000."

MAN: "Well, then go ahead and give them an offer, but just offer $900,000."

WOMAN: "OK. I'll see you later! I love you!"

MAN: "Bye, I love you, too."

The man hangs up. The other men in the locker room are looking at him in astonishment.

Then he asks: "Anyone know who this phone belongs to?"

<u>Mechanics are for Headbangers only!</u>

A couple drove their car to the supermarket only to have their car break down in the car park.

The man told his wife to carry on with the shopping while he fixed the car there and then.

The wife returned later to see a small group of people near the car.

On closer inspection she saw a pair of male legs protruding from under the chassis. Although the man was in shorts, his lack of underpants turned his private parts into glaringly public ones.

Unable to stand the embarrassment she dutifully stepped forward, quickly put her hand UP his shorts and tucked everything back into place. On regaining her feet she looked across the hood and found herself staring at her husband who was standing idly by the car.

The mechanic, however, had to have three stitches in his head.

Escaped prisoner

A man escapes from a prison where he had been kept for 15 years. As he runs away, he finds a house and breaks into it looking for money and guns but only finds a young couple in bed.
He orders the guy out of bed and ties him up in a chair.
While tying the girl up to the bed he gets on top of her, kisses her on the neck, then gets up, and goes to the bathroom.

While he's in there, the husband tells his wife: "Listen, this guy is an escaped prisoner, look at his clothes! He probably spent lots of time in jail, and hasn't seen a woman in years. I saw how he kissed your neck.
If he wants sex, don't resist, don't complain, just do what he tells you,
just give him satisfaction, no matter how much he ravages you.
This guy must be dangerous, if he gets angry, he'll kill us.
Be strong, honey. I love you"

To which the wife responds,
"He wasn't kissing my neck. He was whispering in my ear.
He told me he was gay, thought you were cute, and asked if we kept any Vaseline in the bathroom.

Be strong, honey. I love you, too."

The Best Italiano Shoes

Giorgio has been in the country for about 6 months. He walks to work every day and passes a shoe store. Each day he stops and looks in the window and admires a certain pair of Bocceli leather shoes. After 2 months he saves the £500.00 the shoes cost and purchases them.

Each Friday night the Italian community gets together at a dance at the church basement, so Giorgio seizes the opportunity to wear his new Bocceli leather shoes to the dance.

He first asks Sophia to dance, and as they dance, he asks her, "Sophia, do you wear red panties tonight?" Sophia, startled, says, "Yes, Giorgio, I do wear red panties tonight, but how do you know?!?" Giorgio replies: "I see the reflection in my new £500.00 Bocceli leather shoes. How do you like them?"

Next, he asks Rosa to dance. After a few minutes he says to her, "Rosa, do you wear white panties tonight?" Rosa, startled, answers, "Yes, Giorgio, I do, but how do you know that?!?" He answers: "I see the reflection in my new £500.00 Bocceli leather shoes. How do you like them?"

Now the evening is almost over and the last song is being played. Giorgio asks Carmella to dance. Midway through the dance his face turns red. He says, "Carmella, stilla my heart, please, please tell me you wear no panties tonight. Please, please, tella me this true."

Carmella, embarrassed, answers, "Y... Yes, Giorgio, I wear no panties tonight, but how do you know?!?"

Giorgio gasps and says, "Thanka God... I thought I had a crack in my £500.00 Bocceli leather shoes!!!"

Olympic Condoms!

A man is out shopping and discovers a new brand of Olympic condoms. Clearly impressed, he buys a pack.

Upon getting home he announces to his wife the purchase he just made. Olympic condoms?", she blurts, "What makes them so special?"
There are three colours", he replies, "Gold, Silver and Bronze."

What colour are you going to wear tonight?", she asks cheekily.
Gold of course", says the man proudly.

The wife responds, "Why don't you wear Silver dear, it would be nice if you came second for a change!".

~~~~~~

To all you Virgins out there...........

Thanks for nothing!

MR. FIXIT !

A guy is at home watching the football, when his wife interrupts!

"Could you fix the fridge door? It won't close properly."
"Fix the fridge door?" "Does it look like I have Zanussi written on my forehead? I don't think so."

"Fine!" she says, "Then could you at least re-varnish the front door? It kooks terrible"

"Does it look like I've got Ronseal written on my forehead? I don't think so. I've had enough of this, I'm going to the pub!"

So he goes to the pub and drinks for a couple of hours. When he arrives home, he notices that the steps are fixed. He goes to the fridge to get a beer and notices that the fridge door is also fixed.

"Honey, how'd this all get fixed?"

"Well" she says, "when you left, I sat outside and cried. Just then a nice and very handsome young man asked me what was wrong, so I told him. He offered to do all the repairs, and all I had to do was bake him a cake OR have sex with him."

" So what kind of cake did you bake him?", He asked.

She replied: "HELLO!!!...
Do you see Mr Kipling written on my forehead?
I don't think so!!"

JUST A GLINT OF HUMAN KINDNESS....

This will warm your heart...just when you lost faith in human kindness:

Someone who teaches at a Middle School in Hudson, Florida forwarded the following letter. This letter was sent to the principal's office after the school sponsored a luncheon for the elderly. This story is a credit to all human kind. Read it and show it to all those who could use a lift.

Dear Hudson Middle School,
God blesses you for the beautiful radio that I won at your recent senior citizen's luncheon. I am 84 years old and live at the Hudson Assisted Home for the Aged. All of my family has passed away. I am all-alone now and it's nice to know that someone is thinking of me. God bless you for your kindness to an old forgotten lady.

My roommate is 95 and always had her own radio, but before I received one, she would never let me listen to hers, even when she was napping.
The other day her radio fell off the table and broke into hundreds of pieces.
It was awful and she was in tears.
She asked if she could listen to mine and I said fuck you!
Life is Good.

Sincerely,
Mabel Winters

WAITER, WAITER, There's a Spoon in your Pocket

A timeless lesson on how consultants can make a difference for an organization...

Last week, we took some friends out to a new restaurant, and noticed that the waiter who took our order carried a spoon in his shirt pocket.

It seemed a little strange. When the busboy brought our water and utensils, I noticed he also had a spoon in his shirt pocket. Then I looked around I saw that all the staff had spoons in their pockets.

When the waiter came back to serve our soup I asked, "Why the spoon?"

"Well," he explained, "the restaurant's owners hired a consulting firm to revamp all our processes.

After several months of analysis, they concluded that the spoon was the most frequently dropped utensil. It represents a drop frequency of approximately 3 spoons per table per hour. If our personnel are better prepared, we can reduce the number of trips back to the kitchen and save 15 man-hours per shift."

As luck would have it, I dropped my spoon and he was able to replace it with his spare. "I'll get another spoon next time I go to the kitchen instead of making an extra trip to get it right now."

I was impressed!

I also noticed that there was a string hanging out of the waiter's fly. Looking around, I noticed that all the waiters had the same string hanging from their flies. So before he walked off, I asked the waiter, "Excuse me, but can you tell me why you have that string right there?"

"Oh, certainly!" Then he lowered his voice. "Not everyone is so observant. That consulting firm I mentioned also found out that we could save time in the restroom. By tying this string to the tip of you know what, we can pull it out without touching it and eliminate the need to wash our hands, shortening the time spent in the restroom by 76.39 percent."

That sounded a good idea, but I was puzzled...........

"Hey that's clever, but after you get it out, how do you put it back?"

"Well," he whispered, "I don't know about the others, but I use the spoon."

SEX FROGS!

A beautiful, well-endowed, young blonde goes to her local pet store in search of an exotic pet.

As she looks about the store, she notices box full of frogs. The sign says: "Sex" Frogs! Only £20 each! Money Back Guarantee! (Comes with complete instructions).

The girl excitedly looks around to see if anybody's watching her and whispers softly to the man behind the counter, "I'll take one." The man packaged the frog and said, "Just follow the instructions carefully."

The girl nods, grabs the box, & is quickly on her way home.
As soon as she closes the door to her apartment, the girl takes out the instructions and reads them thoroughly, doing
exactly what it says to do.

1. Take a shower.
2. Splash on some nice smelling perfume.
3. Slip into a very sexy teddy.
4. Crawl into bed and put the frog down "there".

She then quickly gets into bed with the frog and, to her surprise, nothing happens! The girl is totally frustrated and quite upset at this point. She re-reads the instructions and notices at the bottom of the paper it says,   "If you have any problems or questions, please call the pet store." So, the girl calls the pet store. The owner says, "I had a complaint about this particular frog yesterday. I'll be right over."

Within five minutes, the man is ringing her doorbell. The girl welcomes him in and says, "See, I've done everything according to the instructions and the damn thing just sits there."
The man, looking very concerned, picks up the frog, stares directly into its eyes and sternly says:

"Listen to me! I'm only going to show you how to do this one more time.

Remember those Fortune Cookies in Chinese Restaurants?

Thought For The Day:

Isn't it a bit unnerving that doctors call what they do "practice?"

Colonel Sanders?

Sometimes it DOES take a Rocket Scientist!! (true story)

Scientists at Roll Royce built a gun specifically to launch dead chickens at the windshields of airliners, and military jets, all travelling at maximum velocity. The idea is to simulate the frequent incidents of collisions with airborne fowl to test the strength of the windshields.

American engineers heard about the gun and were eager to test it on the windshields of their new high speed trains. Arrangements were made, and a gun was sent to the American engineers. When the gun was fired, the engineers stood shocked as the chicken hurled out of the barrel, crashed into the shatterproof shield, smashed it to smithereens, blasted through the control console, snapped the engineer's back-rest in two and embedded itself in the back wall of the cabin, like an arrow shot from a bow.

The horrified Yanks sent Rolls Royce the disastrous results of the experiment, along with the designs of the windshield and begged the British scientists for suggestions.

Rolls Royce responded with a one-line memo:

"Defrost the chicken."

<u>What Really Happens in our Hospitals!</u>

A nurse told this story.... and she swears this really happened in her ward.

A man suspected of SARS is lying in bed with a mask over his mouth.
A young auxiliary nurse appears to sponge his face and hands.
Nurse," he mumbles from behind the mask," Are my testicles black?"

Embarrassed the young nurse replies, "I don't know Mr Brown, I'm only here to wash your face and hands.

He struggles again to ask, "Nurse, Are my testicles black?"

Again the nurse replies, "I can't tell. I'm only here to wash your face and hands."
The Head Nurse was passing and saw the man getting a little distraught, so she marched over to inquire what was wrong.

"Nurse," he mumbled, "Are my testicles black?"
Being a nurse of long-standing, the Head Nurse was undaunted.
She whipped back the bedclothes, pulled down his pyjama trousers, moved his penis out of the way, had a right good look, pulled up the pyjamas, replaced the bedclothes and announced, "Nothing wrong with your testicles!!!"

At this, the man pulled off his mask and asked again,
"I SAID!!!!!: Are my test results back???"

Old Age Cinders

Cinderella was now 75 years old. After a fulfilling life with the now departed Prince, she happily sat in her rocking chair watching the world go by with her cat Alan. One afternoon, out of nowhere, appeared her Fairy Godmother. Cinderella said, "Fairy Godmother, what are you doing here after all these years?"

The Fairy Godmother replied, "Well Cinderella, since you have lived a good wholesome life since we last met, I have decided to grant you three wishes. Is there anything for which your heart still yearns?"

Cinderella was overjoyed. "I wish I was extremely wealthy", she said.

Instantly, her rocking chair turned into solid gold. Alan, her cat, jumped off her lap and ran to the edge of the porch quivering with fear.

"Oh thank you Fairy Godmother," said Cinderella.

"Is there anything else you might wish for", asked the Fairy Godmother.

Cinderella looked down at her frail body, and said, "I wish I was young and full of the beauty I once had." At once, her wish was granted. Cinderella felt that feeling inside her that she had not felt for years.

The Fairy Godmother said, "You have one wish remaining, what shall you have?"

Cinderella looked at her frightened cat in the corner and said, "I wish for you to turn Alan, my old cat, into a handsome young man."

Magically, Alan suddenly underwent a change and then before them stood a young man with the looks and body that no other man could match. The Fairy Godmother again spoke "Congratulations Cinderella. Enjoy your new life," and with that she was gone.

For a few eerie moments, Cinderella and Alan looked into each other's eyes. Cinderella sat breathless, gazing at the most stunning, perfect man she had ever seen. Then Alan walked over to Cinderella and held her close in his muscular arms. He leant in close to her ear and whispered in a warm breath, "bet you regret having my balls chopped off now, don't you?"

9 IMPORTANT MEN IN WOMEN'S LIVES

1. THE DOCTOR : Says, "Take your clothes off."

2. THE DENTIST : Says, "Open wide."

3. THE HAIRDRESSER : Says," Do you want it teased or blown?".

4. THE MILKMAN : Says, "Do you want cream today?"

5. THE INTERIOR DECORATOR: Says, "Once it's in, you'll love it!"

6. THE STOCK BROKER : Says, "It will rise right up, fluctuate for a while, and then slowly fall back again."

7. THE BANKER : Says, "If you take it out too soon, you'll lose interest.

8. THE HUNTER : Goes deep in the bush, shoots twice, and always eats what he shoots.

9. THE TELEPHONE GUY : Says, "Would you like it on the table or up against the wall.

~~~~~~~~~~~~~~~~~~~~~~~~~~~~

CONSCIOUSNESS:

That annoying time between naps

Snappy Answer #1

A flight attendant was stationed at the departure gate to check tickets.
As a man approached, she extended her hand for the ticket, but he opened his trench coat and flashed her.

Without missing a beat she said, "Sir, I need to see your ticket, not your stub."

~~~~~~

IT'S A FINE TIME FOR THAT MALARKY!

Sheila the Aussie housewife got out of the shower and slipped over on the bathroom floor.
Instead of slipping over forwards or backwards, she somehow slipped
sideways and did the splits and suctioned herself to the floor. She yelled out for her husband Bruce.
"Bruce! Bruce!" she yelled. Bruce came running in.
"Bruce, I've bloody suctioned myself to the floor," she said.
"Strewth!" Bruce said and tried to pull her up. "You're stuck fast girl. I'll go across the road and get Ralph." (his mate).

They both tried to pull her up with no success. After a good look and assessment of the situation, Ralph said "Let's try Plan B."
"Plan B?!" exclaimed Bruce. "What's that?"

"I'll go home and get my hammer and chisel and we'll break the tiles underneath her," replied Ralph.

"Aah Brill!." said Bruce.

When Ralph came back, he was startled to see Bruce playing with his wife's tits.
Ralph said, "Not exactly a good time for playing with her tits mate."

"No," Bruce replied, "But I've been thinking and these tiles were damned expensive and I reckon if I can get her wet enough, we can slide her into the kitchen on to the cheaper tiles."

I SHALL SEEK AND FIND YOU

I SHALL TAKE YOU TO BED,
AND CONTROL YOU

I WILL MAKE YOU ACHE,
SHAKE, AND SWEAT

UNTIL YOU MOAN AND
GROAN...

ALL MY LOVE

THE FLU

Snappy Answer #2

A lady was picking through the frozen turkeys at the grocery store, but couldn't find one big enough for her family. She asked a stock boy, "Do these turkeys get any bigger?" The stock boy replied, "No ma'am, they're dead."

~~~~~~~~~~~~~~~~~~~~~~~~~~~~~~~~~~~~

Betting Man

A man is sitting reading his newspaper when the wife sneaks up behind him and whacks him on the head with a frying pan.

"What was that for?" he asks.

"That was for the piece of paper in your trouser pockets with the name Mary Ellen written on it," she replies.

"Don't be silly," he says. "Two weeks ago when I went to the races, Mary Ellen was the name of one of the horses I bet on."

She seems satisfied and at this, she apologizes.

Three days later he's again sitting in his chair reading when she nails him with an even bigger frying pan, knocking him out cold.

When he comes around, he asks again, "what was what for?!"

She responded, "Your horse phoned."

Hair today............

A senior citizen's group chartered a bus from Brooklyn to Atlantic City. As they entered New Jersey, an elderly woman came up to the driver and said "I've been molested!"

The driver thought she was just being delusional, and told her to go sit back down.
 10 minutes later, another old woman came forward and claimed SHE'D been molested. The driver thought he had a bus load of wackos - who'd molest them?
 10 minutes later, a third came up and said she'd been molested too. The driver decided he'd had enough, and pulled into the rest stop. When he stood up, he saw an old man on his hands and knees in the aisle.

"Hey gramps, what are you doing down there?"

"I lost my toupee. Three times I thought I found it, but when I grabbed it, it ran away...

Snappy Answer #3

The cop got out of his car and the kid who was stopped for speeding
pulled down his window. "I've been waiting for you all day," the cop said. The kid replied, "Yeah, well I got here as fast as I could." When the cop finally stopped laughing, he sent the kid on his way without a ticket.

IRELAND – The Golfer and the Leprechaun

A golfer in Ireland hit a bad hook into the woods. Looking for the ball,
he discovered a Leprechaun flat on his back, a big bump on his head, and the
golfer's ball beside him. Horrified, the golfer took his water bottle
from his belt and poured it over the little guy, reviving him.

"Arrgh! What happen?" the leprechaun says. "Oh, I see. Waal, ye got me
fair and square. Ye get three wishes. Whaddya want?"

"Thank God, you're all right!" the golfer answers in relief.

"I don't want anything. I'm glad you're okay, and I apologize. I didn't
mean to hit you." And the golfer walks off.

"What a nice guy," the leprechaun says to himself. "But it was fair and
 square that he got me, and I have to do something for him.
 I'll give him three things I would want --- a great golf game, all the
money he ever needs, and a fantastic sex life."

A year goes by and the golfer is back, hits another bad ball into the
woods and finds the leprechaun waiting for him.

"'Twas me that made ye hit the ball here," the little guy says. "I wanted
to ask ye, how's yer golf game?"

"That's the first bad ball I've hit in a year! I'm a famous international
golfer now," the golfer answers. "By the way, it's good to see you're all
right."

"Oh, I'm fine now, thankee. I did that fer yer golf game. And tell me, hows
yer money?"

"Why, I win fortunes in golf. But if I need cash,
I just reach in my pocket and pull out $100 bills all day long."

"I did that fer ye. And how's yer sex life?"

"The golfer blushes, turns his head away in embarrassment, and says shyly
"Errr, all right, I suppose."

 "C'mon, c'mon now. I want to know if I did a good job. How many
times a day?"

Blushing even more, the golfer whispers, "Once-- sometimes twice a week."

"What!" says the leprechaun in shock? "That's all? Once or twice a week?"

"Well," says the golfer, "I figure that's not too bad for a Catholic
priest in a small parish!"

OPERATION NERVES?

Two little boys are in a hospital, lying on stretchers next to each other, outside the operating room. The first kid leans over and asks, "What are you in here for?" The second kid says, "I'm in here to get my tonsils out and I'm a little nervous. The first kid says, "You've got nothing to worry about. I had that done when I was four.
They put you to sleep, and when you wake up they give you lots of Jelly and ice cream. It's a breeze."

The second kid then asks, "What are you here for?" The first kid says,
"A Circumcision." And the second kid says,
"Whoa, Good luck buddy, I had that done when I was born. Couldn't walk for a year."

~~~~~~~~~~~~~~~~~

Prayer:

One of the prayers overheard at Old Age Homes Toilets:
A 75-year-old man talking to his penis.

We were born together

Grew up together

Had a lot of fun together

Enjoyed life together

So now, <u>why</u> did you die before me?

WOMEN – VERY CLEVER!

A woman and a man are involved in a car accident; it's a bad one.
Both of their cars are totally demolished but amazingly neither of
them are hurt.
After they crawl out of their cars, the woman says, "So you're a man
That's interesting. I'm a woman.
Wow, just look at our cars!
There's nothing left, but we're unhurt. This must be a sign from
God that we should meet and be friends and live together in peace
for the rest of our days".

Flattered, the man replied, "Oh yes, I agree with you completely!"
"This must be a sign from God!"
The woman continued, "and look at this, here's another miracle.
My car is completely demolished but this bottle of wine didn't break.
Surely God wants us to drink this wine and celebrate our good
fortune."
Then she hands the bottle to the man.
The man nods his head in agreement, opens it and drinks half the
bottle and then hands it back to the woman. The woman takes the
bottle and immediately puts the cap back on, and hands it back to
the man.

The man asks, "Aren't you having any?"
The woman replies, "No. I think I'll just wait for the police...."

MORAL OF THE STORY:

Women are clever bitches. Don't mess with them.

What do you call a fish with no eyes?
A fsh.

(Thanks go to DS of Maidenhead for this gem)

~~~~~~~~~~~~~~~~~

Sometimes I wake up grumpy...
Other times I let him sleep

~~~~~~~~~~~~~~~~~

I want to die in my sleep like my grandfather...
Not yelling and screaming like the passengers in his car!

Actual Newspaper Headline:

Juvenile Court to Try Shooting Defendant

What's in a name?

A psychiatrist was conducting a group therapy session with four young mothers and their small children... "You all have obsessions," he observed.

To the first mother, he said, "You are obsessed with eating. You've even named your daughter Candy."

He turned to the second Mum. Your obsession is with money. Again, it manifests itself in your child's name, Penny."

He turns to the third Mum. "Your obsession is alcohol. This too manifests itself in your child's name, Brandy."

At this point, the fourth mother gets up, takes her little boy by the hand and whispers.
"Come on, Dick, we're leaving.

~~~~~~~~~~~~~~~~~~~~~~~~~~~~~

LOST

A small boy was lost at a large shopping mall.

He approached a uniformed policeman and said, "I've lost my dad!"
The cop asked, "What's he like?"
The little boy replied, "Beer, and women with big tits."

Another Genie Story...........

A man is walking down a beach, and accidentally kicks a bottle out of
the sand. He opens the bottle, and a genie appears.
The genie said, "I am so grateful to get out of that bottle that I will
grant you one wish. But I can only grant one."

The man thought for a while and finally said, "I have always wanted
to go to Hawaii.

I've never been able to go because airplanes are much too frightening
for me and boats make me seasick. So I wish for a road to be built
from here to Hawaii."

The genie thought for a few minutes and said, "No, I can't do it.
Imagine all the work involved. All the piling to hold up the highway
needed and the entire pavement. Ask for something else."

"Well," the man said. "I would like to be able to understand women.
What makes them laugh and cry, why are they temperamental, why
are they so difficult to get along with. Basically, what makes them
tick?

The genie considered this for a couple of minutes and said, "So, do
you want two lanes or four?

Never forget to "Think Outside of the Box."

You are driving along in your car on a wild, stormy night.
You pass by a bus stop, and you see three people waiting for the bus:
　　1. An old lady who looks as if she is about to die.
　　2. An old friend who once saved your life.
　　3. The perfect partner you have been dreaming about.
Which one would you choose to offer a ride to; knowing that there could only be one passenger in your car.
Think before you continue reading.

This is a moral/ethical dilemma that was once actually used as part of a job application.
You could pick up the old lady, because she is going to die, and thus you should save her first; or you could take the old friend because he once saved your life, and this would be the perfect chance to pay him back.
However, you may never be able to find your perfect dream lover again.
The candidate who was hired (out of 2000 applicants) had no trouble coming up with an answer.

WHAT DID HE SAY?

He simply answered: "I would give the car keys to my old friend, and let him take the lady to the hospital. And I would stay behind and wait for the bus with the woman of my dreams."
Sometimes, we gain more if we are able to give up our stubborn thought limitations.

Never forget to "Think Outside of the Box."

However, the correct answer is to run the old lady over and put her out of her misery, shag the perfect partner against the bus stop and drive off for a beer with the old friend!

A Day At The Nudist Beach

A mother and father took their 6-year-old son to a nudist beach. As the boy walked along the beach, he noticed that some of the ladies had boobs bigger than his mother's and asked her why.

She told her son, "The bigger they are the dumber the person is."

The boy, pleased with the answer, goes to play in the ocean but returns to tell his mother that many of the men have larger willies than his dad. His mother replied, "The bigger they are the dumber the person is."

Again satisfied with this answer, the boy returns to the ocean to play.

Shortly after, the boy returned again. He promptly tells his mother, "Daddy is talking to the dumbest girl on the beach and the longer he talks, the dumber <u>he</u> gets."

~~~~~~

Please Help Me I'm Falling

When O' Conner fell a hundred feet from a building site he was asked if he was hurt by the fall.
"Well no, not really" he replied... It wasn't the fall that hurt me so much as the landing."

T.O.U.C.H.E.

Three guys and a lady were sitting at the bar talking about their professions.

The first guy says, "I'm a **Y.U.P.P.I.E**,
You know...**Young, Urban, Professional, Peaceful, Intelligent, Ecologist**."

The second guy says, "Hey, well I'm a **D.I.N.K.Y**., you know...
Double Income, No Kids Yet."

The third guy says, "That makes me a **R.U.B**. then; you know...
Rich, Urban, Biker"

They turn to a woman sitting close by and ask her, "And how would you describe yourself"

She replies: "I'm a **WIFE**,

You know... **Wash, Iron, Fuck, Etc.**"

Actual Newspaper Headlines:

Police Begin Campaign to Run Down Jaywalkers

Something Went Wrong in Jet Crash, Expert Says

Plastic Mac?

A woman was having a daytime affair while her husband was at work.

One wet and lusty day she was in bed with her boyfriend when, to her horror, she heard her husband's car pull into the driveway. "Oh My God - Hurry! grab your clothes," she yelled to her lover. "And jump out the window. My husband's home early!"

I can't jump out the window!" came the strangled reply from beneath the sheets "It's raining out there!" "If my husband catches us in here, he'll kill us both!" she replied.

He's got a very quick temper and a very large gun! The rain is the least of your problems"

So the boyfriend scoots out of bed , grabs his clothes and jumps out the window! As he began running down the street in the pouring rain, he quickly discovered he had run right into the middle of the town's annual marathon.

So he started running along beside the others about 300 of them. Being naked, with his clothes tucked under his arm, he tried to "blend in" as best he could. It wasn't that effective!

After a little while, a small group of runners, who had been studying him with some curiosity, jogged closer.

"Do you always run in the nude?" one asked.

"Oh yes" he replied, gasping in air. "It feels so wonderfully free having the air blow over all your skin while you're running."

Another runner moved alongside. "Do you always run carrying your clothes with you under your arm?"

"Oh, yes" our friend answered breathlessly. "That way I can get dressed right at the end of the run and get in my car to go home!"

Then a third runner cast his eyes a little lower and queried. "Do you always wear a condom when you run?"

"Only if it's raining."

No Sex Since 1955!

A crusty old Marine Corps colonel found himself at a gala event downtown, hosted by a local liberal arts college. There was no shortage of extremely young, idealistic ladies in attendance; one of who approached the colonel for conversation.

She said, "excuse me, sir, but you seem to be a very serious, man. Are you this way all the time, or is something bothering you?"

"No," the colonel said, "just serious by nature!"

The young lady looked at his awards and decorations, and said, "It looks like you have seen a lot of action."

The colonel's short reply was, "yes, a lot of action."

The young lady, tiring of trying to start up a conversation, said: "you know, you should lighten up a little.....relax and enjoy yourself."

The colonel just stared at her in his serious manner.

Finally the young lady said, "You know, I hope you don't take this the wrong way, but when is the last time you had sex?"

The colonel looked at her and replied, "1955."

She said, "well there you go, you really need to chill out and quit taking everything so seriously......I mean, no sex since 1955, isn't that a little extreme?"

The colonel, glancing at his watch, said in his matter-of-fact voice, "oh, I don't know, it's only 21.30 now."

THE REAL PHILOSOPHY OF LIFE

A philosophy professor stood before his class and had some items in front of him. When the class began, wordlessly, he picked up a large empty mayonnaise jar and proceeded to fill it with rocks - rocks about 2" in diameter.

He then asked the students if the jar was full. They agreed that it was.

So the professor then picked up a box of small pebbles and poured them into the jar. He shook the jar lightly. The pebbles, of course, rolled into the open areas between the rocks.

He then asked the students again if the jar was full. They agreed. The students laughed. The professor then picked up a box of sand and poured it into the jar. Of course, the sand filled up everything else.

"Now," said the professor, "I want you to recognize that this is your life. The rocks are the important things - your family, your health, your children - things that if everything else were lost and only they remained, your life would still be full. The pebbles are the other things that matter, such as your job, your house, your car. The sand is everything else, the small stuff. If you put the sand into the jar first, there's no room for the pebbles or the rocks. The same goes for your life. If you spend all your time and energy on the small stuff, you'll never have room for the things that are important to you. Pay attention to the things that are critical to your happiness. Play with your children. Take time to get medical checkups. There'll always be time to work, clean the house, give a dinner party and fix the boiler. Take care of the rocks first - the things that really matter. Set your priorities. The rest is just sand."

But then a student took the jar, which the other students and the professor agreed was full, and proceeded to pour in a glass of beer. Of course the beer filled the remaining spaces and soaked into the sand within the jar, making the jar truly full.

The student looked at the class and the professor and added...

"And furthermore this proves that no matter how full your life is, there's always room for a beer"

ANCIENT CHINESE TORTURE

A young man is wandering, lost in a forest, when he comes upon a small house. Knocking on the door he is greeted by an ancient Chinese man with a long beard. "I'm lost," said the young man, "Can you put me up for the night?"

"Certainly," the Chinese man said, "but on one condition. If you so much as lay a finger on my daughter, I will inflict upon you the three worst Chinese tortures known to man." "Ok," said the man, thinking that the daughter must be pretty old as well, and entered the house.

Over dinner, the daughter came down the stairs. She was young, beautiful and had a fantastic body. She was obviously attracted to the young man, since she couldn't keep her eyes off him during the meal.
Remembering the old man's warning, he ignored her and went up to bed alone.
During the night he could bear it no longer and sneaked into her room for a night of passion. He was careful to keep everything quiet so the old man wouldn't hear and, near dawn, he crept back to his room, exhausted but happy.
He woke to feel a pressure on his chest. Opening his eyes, he saw a large rock on his chest with a note on it that read:
"Chinese torture #1: Large rock on chest."
Well, that's pretty lousy torture," he thought.
"If that's the best the old man can do then I don't have much to worry about."
 He picked the boulder up, walked over to the window and threw the boulder out. As he did so, he noticed another note on it that read...
"Chinese torture #2: Rock tied to left testicle."
Panicking, he glanced down and saw that the rope was getting close to taut. Figuring that a few broken bones were better than castration, he jumped out of the window after the boulder.
As he plummeted towards earth, he saw a large sign on the ground that read...
"Chinese torture #3: Right testicle tied to bed post."

50's, 60's and 70's Kids

According to today's regulators and bureaucrats, those of us who were kids in the 50's, 60's, and 70's probably shouldn't have survived, because......

Our baby cots were covered with brightly coloured lead-based paint which was promptly chewed and licked.
We had no childproof lids on medicine bottles, or latches on doors on cabinets and it was fine to play with pans.

When we rode our bikes, we wore no helmets, just flip flops and fluorescent 'clackers' on our wheels.

As children, we would ride in cars with no seat belts or air bags. Riding in the passenger seat was a treat.

We drank water from the garden hose and not from a bottle - tasted the same.

We ate dripping sandwiches, bread and butter pudding and drank fizzy pop with sugar in it, but we were never overweight because we were always outside playing.

We shared one drink with four friends, from one bottle or can and no one actually died from this.

We would spend hours building go-carts out of scraps and then went top speed down the hill, only to find out we forgot the brakes. After running into stinging nettles a few times, we learned to solve the problem.

We would leave home in the morning and play all day, as long as we were back before it got dark. No one was able to reach us all day and no one minded.

We did not have Play stations or X-Boxes, no video games at all. No 99 channels on TV, no videotape movies, no surround sound, no mobile phones, no personal computers, no Internet chat rooms. We had friends - we went outside and found

We fell out of trees, got cut and broke bones and teeth, and there were no lawsuits. They were accidents. We learnt not to do the same thing again.

We had fights, punched each other hard and got black and blue - we learned to get over it.

We walked to friends' homes.

We made up games with sticks and tennis balls and ate live stuff, and although we were told it would happen, we did not have very many eyes out, nor did the live stuff live inside us forever.

We rode bikes in packs of 7 and wore our coats by only the hood.

Our actions were our own. Consequences were expected.

The idea of a parent bailing us out if we broke a law was unheard of. They actually sided with the law. Imagine that!

This generation has produced some of the best risk-takers, problem solvers and inventors, ever. The past 50 years have been an explosion of innovation and new ideas. We had freedom, failure, success and responsibility, and we learned how to deal with it all.

If you're one of them, Congratulations!

Show this to others who have had the luck to grow up as real kids, before lawyers and government regulated our lives, for our own good.

(If you aren't old enough, thought you might like to read about us......)

Expensive Hotel

A husband and wife are travelling by car from Key West to Boston. After almost twenty-four hours on the road, they're too tired to continue, and they decide to stop for a rest. They stop at a nice hotel and take a room, but they only plan to sleep for four hours and then get back on the road.

When they check out four hours later, the desk clerk hands them a bill for $350.

The man explodes and demands to know why the charge is so high. He tells the clerk although it's a nice hotel, the rooms certainly aren't worth $350.

When the clerk tells him $350 is the standard rate, the man insists on speaking to the Manager.

The Manager appears, listens to the man, and then explains that the hotel has an Olympic- sized pool and a huge conference centre that were available for the husband and wife to use.

"But we didn't use them", the man complains. "Well, they are here, and you could have," explains the Manager.

He goes on to explain they could have taken in one of the shows for which the hotel is famous. "The best entertainers from New York, Hollywood and Las Vegas perform here," the Manager says. "But we didn't go to any of those shows," complains the man again.

"Well, we have them, and you could have", the Manager replies. No matter what facility the Manager mentions, the man replies, "But we didn't use it!"

The Manager is unmoved, and eventually the man gives up and agrees to pay.

He writes a cheque and gives it to the Manager. The Manager is surprised when he looks at the cheque. "But sir," he says, "this cheque is only made out for $100."

"That's right," says the man. "I charged you $250 for sleeping with my wife."

"But I didn't!" exclaims the Manager.

"Well," the man replies, "she was here, and you could have."

President Bush

President Bush and Dick Cheney are enjoying a lunch at a fancy Washington restaurant.

Their waitress approaches their table to take their order; she is young and very attractive.
She asks Cheney what he wants, and he replies, "I'll have the heart-healthy salad."
"Very good, sir," she replies, and turning to Bush she asks, "And what do you want, Mr. President?"
Bush answers, "How about a quickie?"
Taken aback, the waitress slaps him and says, "I'm shocked and disappointed in you. I thought you were bringing in a new administration that was committed to high principles and morality.
I'm sorry I voted for you."
With that, the waitress departed in a huff.

Cheney leans over to Bush, and says,
"Mr. President, I believe that's pronounced 'quiche.'"

~~~~~~~~~~~~~~~~~~~~~~~~~~~~

Snappy Answer #4

A truck driver was driving along on the freeway. A sign comes up that reads "low bridge ahead." Before he knows it the bridge is right ahead of him and he gets stuck under the bridge. Cars are backed up for miles. Finally, a police car comes up. The cop gets out of his car and walks around to the truck driver, puts his hands on his hips and says, "Got stuck, heh?" The truck driver says, "No, I was delivering this bridge and ran out of gas."

The Free Kick Rule?

An Australian went duck shooting whilst on holiday in NZ. He shot and dropped a bird, but it fell into a farmer's field on the other side of a fence. As the Aussie climbed over the fence, an elderly farmer drove by on his tractor and asked him what he was doing. The Aussie responded, "I shot a duck and it fell into this field, and now I'm going to retrieve it." The old farmer replied, "This is my property, and you are not coming over here." The indignant Aussie said, "Listen, here mate, I am one of the best trial lawyers in Australia, if you don't let me get that duck, I'll sue you and take everything you own. The old farmer smiled and said, "Apparently, you don't know how we do things here. We settle small disagreements like this with the Three Kick Rule."

The Aussie asked, "What the hell is the Three Kick Rule?"

The Farmer replied, "Well, first I kick you three times and then you kick me three times and so on back and forth until someone gives up."

The Aussie quickly thought about the proposed contest and decided that he could easily take the old codger. He agreed to abide by the local custom.

The old farmer slowly climbed down from the tractor and walked up to the Aussie.

His first kick planted the toe of his heavy work boot into the Aussie's groin and dropped him to his knees.

His second kick to the midriff sent the Aussie's last meal gushing from his mouth.

The Aussie was on all fours when the farmer's third kick to his rear end sent him face-first into a fresh cowpat. The Aussie summoned every bit of his will and managed to get to his feet.

Wiping his face with the arm of his expensive jacket, he said, "Okay, you old coot. Now it's my turn."

The old farmer smiled and said,

"Nah, I give up. You can have the duck."

<u>The Amazing Claude</u>!

It was opening night at the Orpheum, and the Amazing Claude was topping the bill.
People came from miles around to see the famed hypnotist do his stuff.
As Claude took to the stage, he announced, "Unlike most stage hypnotists who invite two or three people up onto the stage to be put into a trance, I intend to hypnotise each and every member of the audience."

The excitement was almost electric as Claude withdrew a beautiful antique pocket watch from his coat.

I want you each to keep your eye on this antique watch. It's a very special watch. It's been in my family for six generations.
He began to swing the watch gently back and forth while quietly chanting...
"Watch the watch, watch the watch, watch the watch....

"The crowd became mesmerised as the watch swayed back and forth,
light gleaming off its polished surface.
Hundreds of pairs of eyes followed the swaying watch, when it suddenly slipped from the hypnotist's fingers and fell to the floor, breaking into a hundred pieces.

"Shit!" said the hypnotist.

It took three weeks to clean up the theatre.

<u>WAKEY WAKEY!</u>

A man and his wife were having some problems at home and were giving each other the silent treatment. The next week the man realized that he would need his wife to wake him at 5:00 am for a flight to Europe. Not wanting to be the first to break the silence, he finally wrote on a piece of paper,
"Please wake me tomorrow morning at 5:00 am".

The next morning the man woke up, only to discover it was 9:00am, and that he had missed his flight. Furious, he was about to go and see why his wife hadn't woken him when he noticed a piece of paper by the bed - it said:
"It's 5:00am, wake up".

~~~~~~~~~~~~~~~~~~~~~~~~~~~~~~

Q. What's the definition of macho?

A. Jogging home from your own vasectomy.

<u>REVENGE!</u>

A woman recently lost her husband. She had him
cremated and brought his ashes home.
One day she picked up the urn he was in, and poured him out
on the coffee table.

Then she started talking to him, and tracing her fingers in the
ashes.
She said, "You know that fur coat you promised me Irving?"
I bought it with the insurance money!"
She then said, "Irving, remember that new car you promised
me?
Well, I bought it with the insurance money!"
Then she said, "And remember the big beautiful house that
sits at the top of the hill that I fell in love with and you said
we couldn't afford?
Well I bought that too with the insurance money and I love
living here."

Still tracing her fingers in the ashes, she said,
"Irving, remember that blow job I promised you?
Well............ here it comes..."

Some very famous people answer the question:

Why DID the chicken cross the road? - I

SAEED AL SAHAF - Iraqi Head of Information
The chicken did not cross the road. This is a complete fabrication. We do not even have a chicken.

GEORGE W BUSH
We don't care why the chicken crossed the road. We just want to know if the chicken is on our side of the road or not. The chicken is either for us or against us. There is no middle ground.

COLIN POWELL
Now to the left of the screen, you can clearly see the satellite image of the chicken crossing the road.

TONY BLAIR
I agree with George.

HANS BLIX
We have reason to believe there is a chicken, but we have not yet been allowed to have access to the other side of the road.

DR SEUSS
Did the chicken cross the road?
Did he cross it with a toad?
Yes, the chicken crossed the road,
But why it crossed I've not been told.

<u>Why DID the chicken cross the road?</u> - 2

<u>MARTIN LUTHER KING, JR</u>
I envision a world where all chickens will be free to cross roads without having their motives called into question.

<u>GRANDPA</u>
In my day, we didn't ask why the chicken crossed the road. Somebody told us the chicken crossed the road, and that was good enough.

<u>TRICIA</u>
Isn't that interesting? In a few moments, we will be listening to the chicken tell, for the first time, the heart-warming story of how it experienced a serious case of moulting, and went on to accomplish its dream of crossing the road.

<u>JOHN LENNON</u>
Imagine all the chickens in the world crossing roads together - in peace.

<u>ARISTOTLE</u>
It is the nature of chickens to cross the road.

<u>KARL MARX</u>
It was an historic inevitability.

<u>RONALD REAGAN</u>
What chicken?

Chicken

<u>SIGMUND FREUD</u>
The fact that you are at all concerned that the chicken crossed the road reveals your underlying sexual insecurity.

<u>BILL GATES</u>
eChicken2003 will not only cross roads, but will lay eggs, file your important documents, and balance your cheque book - and internet explorer is an integral part of eChicken.

<u>ALBERT EINSTEIN</u>
Did the chicken really cross the road, or did the road move beneath the chicken?

<u>ARIEL SHARON</u>
Is this chicken kosher?

<u>THE BIBLE</u>
And God came down from heaven, and he said unto the chicken THOU SHALT CROSS THE ROAD. And the chicken didst cross the road, and there was rejoicing.

<u>COLONEL SANDERS</u>
Did I miss one?

<u>HOMER SIMPSON</u>
Mmmmmmmmm .... **c h i c k e n !**

THE HOKEY COKEY

What with all the sadness and trauma going on in the world at the moment
it is worth reflecting on the death of a very important person which almost went un-noticed in February 2003.

Larry La Prise, the man who wrote "The Hokey Cokey" died peacefully at age 93.

The most traumatic part for his family was getting him into the coffin.

They put his left leg in... And then the trouble started.

~~~~~~~~~~~~~~~~~~~~~~~~~~~~

Terrible Clef!

My parents recently retired. Mum always wanted to learn to play the piano, so dad bought her a piano for her birthday. A few weeks later, I asked how she was doing with it. "Oh, we returned the piano." said My Dad, "I persuaded her to switch to a clarinet instead."

"Why?" I asked.

"Because," he answered, "with a clarinet, she can't sing."

Oh No……..

A woman has twins, and gives them up for adoption. One of them goes to a family in Egypt and is named "Amal."

The other goes to a family in Spain, they name him Juan".

Years later, Juan sends a picture of himself to his real mum. Upon receiving the picture, she tells her husband that she wished she also had a picture of Amal.

Her husband responds, "But they are twins. If you've seen Juan, you've seen Amal."

~~~~~~~~~~~~~~~~~~~~~~~~~~~~~~~~~~~~~~

Dumb & Dumber

The proverbial Englishman, Irishman and Scotsman were sitting in a bar when the conversation turned to their wives and how stupid they were.
Each one claimed to have the dumbest wife of all and to settle the argument, they gave an example of their wife's behaviour:

The Scotsman said ' mah wife went oot and bought a DVD player, and we havenae even got a television set ! '
'That's nothing ' said the Englishman. ' My wife won some money at the casino and spent the bloody lot on a car. She hasn't even got a driving licence, and neither have I.'
'Well,' says Paddy, ' my wife booked up a holiday in Italy for herself and her sister. Then she went and bought 100 condoms, and she hasn't even got anything to put them on!

Trunk Call

Jack goes to the doctor and says "Doc I'm having trouble getting my penis erect, can you help me ? "
After a complete examination the doctor tells Jack,
" Well the problem with you is that the muscles around the base of your penis are damaged. There's really nothing I can do for you except if you're willing to try an experimental treatment."
Jack asks sadly, " What is this treatment ? "
" Well," the doctor explains, " what we would do is take the muscles from the trunk of a baby elephant and implant them in your penis."
Jack thinks about it silently then says,
" Well, the thought of going through life without ever having sex again is too much, lets go for it."
A few weeks after the operation Jack was given the green light to use his improved equipment. He planned a romantic evening for his girl friend and took her to one of the nicest restaurants in the city. In the middle of dinner he felt a stirring between his legs that continued to the point of being uncomfortable. To release the pressure Jack unzipped his fly. His penis immediately sprung from his pants, went to the top of the table, grabbed a bread roll and then returned to his pants. His girl friend was stunned at first but then said with a sly smile, " That was incredible! Can you do that again? "

Jack replied, "Well, I guess so, but I'm not sure I can fit another bread roll up my arse! "

Planting Spuds

Old Sean lived alone in Northern Ireland. He wanted to dig his potato garden, but it was very hard work. His only son, Mick, who used to help him, was in an English prison. The old man wrote a letter to his son and described his predicament:

Dear Mick,
I am feeling a mite down because it looks like I won't be able to plant me potato garden this year. I'm just getting too old to be digging up a garden plot. If you were here, all my troubles would be over. I know you would dig the plot for me.
Love, Dad

A few days later he received a letter from his son:

Dear Father,

For CHRIST'S SAKE, don't dig up the garden! That's where I buried all them feckin' BODIES!
Love, Mick

At 4am the next morning, a dozen agents from Scotland Yard and local police officers showed up and dug up the entire garden down to a depth of about six feet. That evening, not finding any bodies, they apologised to the old man and left. The next day the old man received another letter from his son:

Dear Father,
Go ahead and plant yer spuds now. It's the best I could do under the circumstances.
Love, Mick

It's Dark In Here

A woman takes a lover during the day, while her husband is at work. One day, her 9-year-old son hides in the closet during one of her romps. Her husband comes home unexpectedly, so she
hides the lover in the closet.

The little boy says, "It's dark in here."

The man whispers, "Yes, it is."

Boy - "I have a baseball."

Man - "That's nice."

Boy - "Want to buy it?"

Man - "No, thanks."

Boy - "My dad's outside."

Man - "OK, how much?"

Boy - "$250."

In the next few weeks, it happens again that the boy and the mom's lover end up in the closet together.

Boy - "It's dark in here."

Man - "Yes, it is."

Boy - "I have a baseball glove."

Man - Remembering last time, asks, "How much?"

Boy - "$750."

Man - "Fine."

A few days later, the father says to the boy, "Grab your ball and glove. Let's go outside and toss the baseball "

The boy says, "I can't. I sold them."

The father asks, "How much did you sell them for?"

The son says "$1,000."

The father says, "It's terrible to overcharge your friends like that. That's way more than those two things cost. I'm going to take you to church and make you confess."

They go to the church and the father makes the little boy sit in the confession booth and he closes the door.

The boy says, "It's dark in here."

The priest says, "Don't start that sh!t again!"

<u>KIDS ADVICE TO KIDS #1</u>

"Never trust a dog to watch your food."
Patrick, age 10

When your dad is mad and asks you, 'Do I look stupid? Don't answer!"
Hannah, 9

"Never tell your mum her diet's not working."
Michael, 14

"When your mum is mad at your dad, don't let her brush your hair".

Taylia, 10

~~~~~~

Answerphone message

"....If you want to buy marijuana,

press the hash key...."

Grandmas Letter

The other day I went up to a local Christian bookstore and saw a *HONK IF YOU LOVE JESUS* bumper sticker.

I was feeling particularly sassy that day because I had just come from a thrilling choir performance, followed by a thunderous prayer meeting, so I bought the sticker and put in on my bumper.

I was stopped at a red light at a busy intersection, just lost in thought about the Lord and how good He is and I didn't notice that the light had changed..

It is a good thing someone else loves Jesus because if he hadn't honked, I'd never have noticed.

I found that LOTS of people love Jesus. Why, while I was sitting there, the guy behind started honking like crazy, and when he leaned out of his window and screamed, "for the love of God, GO! GO!" What an exuberant cheerleader he was for Jesus.

Everyone started honking! I just leaned out of my window and started waving and smiling at all these loving people..

I even honked my horn a few times to share in the love. There must have been a man from Florida back there because I heard him yelling something about a sunny beach...

I saw another guy waving in a funny way with only his middle finger stuck up in the air. When I asked my teenage grandson in the back seat what that meant, he said that it was probably a Hawaiian good luck sign or something.

Well, I've never met anyone from Hawaii, so I leaned out the window and gave him the good luck sign back.

My grandson burst out laughing, why even he was enjoying this religious experience. A couple of the people were so caught up in the joy of the moment that they got out of their cars and started walking towards me.

I bet they wanted to pray or ask what church I attended, but this is when I noticed the light had changed.

So, I waved to all my sisters and brothers grinning, and drove on through the intersection.

I noticed I was the only car that got through the intersection before the light changed again and I felt kind of sad that I had to leave them after all the love we had shared, so I slowed the car down, leaned out of the window and gave them all the Hawaiian good luck sign one last time as I drove away.

Praise the Lord for such wonderful folks!

Disorder in Court.

Almost unbelievably, these are things people actually said in court, word for word, taken down and now published by court reporters - who had the torment of staying calm while these exchanges were actually taking place.

Q: What is your date of birth?
A: July fifteenth.
Q: What year?
A: Every year.

~~~~~~

Q: What gear were you in at the moment of the impact?
A: Gucci sweats and Reeboks.

~~~~~~

Q: What was the first thing your husband said to you when he woke up that morning?
A: He said, "Where am I, Cathy?"
Q: And why did that upset you?
A: My name is Susan.

~~~~~~

Q: How was your first marriage terminated?
A: By death.
Q: And by whose death was it terminated?

~~~~~~

Q: Doctor, how many autopsies have you performed on dead people?
A: All my autopsies are performed on dead people.
Q: All your responses must be oral, OK?
What school did you go to?
A: Oral.

~~~~~~

Q: Do you recall the time that you examined the body?
A: The autopsy started around 8:30 pm
Q: And Mr. Dennington was dead at the time?
A: No, he was sitting on the table wondering why I was doing an autopsy.

~~~~~~

Q: Doctor, before you performed the autopsy, did you check for a Pulse?
A: No.
Q: Did you check for blood pressure?
A: No.
Q: Did you check for breathing?
A: No.
Q: So, then it is possible that the patient was alive when you began the autopsy?
A: No.
Q: How can you be so sure, Doctor?
A: Because his brain was sitting on my desk in a jar.

Q: But could the patient have still been alive, nevertheless?
A: Well, yes, I suppose it is possible that he could have been alive and practicing law somewhere.

As Alf grew older he began to have trouble with his joints

The President of the United States goes to Hell.......

George Bush has a heart attack and dies. He goes to hell where the devil is waiting for him.

"I don't know what to do here, " says the devil. "You are on my list but I have no room for you. You definitely have to stay here, so I'll tell you what I'm going to do. I've got three folks here who weren't

quite as bad as you. I'll let one of them go, but you have to take their place. I'll even let YOU decide who leaves." George thought that sounded pretty good, so he agreed.

The devil opened the first room: in it was Richard Nixon and a large pool of water. He kept diving in and surfacing empty-handed over and over and over. Such was his fate in hell. "No!" George said. "I don't think so. I'm not a good swimmer and don't think I could do that all day long."

The devil led him to the next room: in it was Tony Blair with a sledgehammer and a room full of rocks. All he did was swing the hammer, time after time after time. "No, I've got this problem with my shoulder. I would be in constant agony if all I could do was break rocks all day!" commented George.

The devil opened a third door. In it, George saw Bill Clinton, lying on the floor with his arms staked over his head, and his legs staked in spread eagle pose. Bent over him was Monica Lewinsky, doing what she does best.

George Bush looked at this in disbelief for a while and finally said ....

"Yeah, I can handle this." The devil smiled and said...........

........"OK, Monica, you're free to go!"

What Are These For Dad?

A man walks into a drug store with his 8-year-old son. They happen to walk by the condom display, and the boy asks,
"What are these, Dad?"
The man matter-of-factly replies, "Those are called condoms, son. Men use them to have safe sex."
"Oh I see," replied the boys pensively. "Yes, I've heard of that in health class at school."

He looks over the display and picks up a package of three and asks, "Why are there three in this package."
The dad replies, "Those are for high-school boys. One for Friday, one for Saturday, and one for Sunday."
"Cool!" says the boy.

He notices a pack of six and asks "Then who are these for?"
"Those are for college men," the dad answers, "Two for Friday, two for Saturday, and two for Sunday."
"Wow!" exclaimed the boy.

"Then who uses these?" he asks, picking up a 12-pack.
With a sigh, the dad replied, "Those are for married men. One for January, one for February, one for March, etc,."

The Next Move

A group of chess enthusiasts checked into a hotel and were standing in the lobby discussing their recent tournament victories. After about an hour, the manager came out of the office and asked them to disperse "But why?" they asked, as they moved off. "Because," he said "I can't stand chess nuts boasting in an open foyer."

QUICKIES!!

There was a man who entered a local paper's pun contest. He sent in ten different puns, in the hope that at least one of the puns would win.
Unfortunately, no pun in ten did

~~~~~~~~~~~~~~~~~~~~~~~~~~~~~~~~~~~~

So I went to the Chinese restaurant and this duck came up to me with a red rose and says "Your eyes sparkle like diamonds". I said "Waiter, I asked for a-ROMATIC duck"

~~~~~~~~~~~~~~~~~~~~~~~~~~~~~~~~~~~~

A three-legged dog walks into a saloon in the Old West. He slides up to the bar and announces: "I'm looking for the man who shot my paw."

~~~~~~~~~~~~~~~~~~~~~~~~~~~~~~~~~~~~

I met a Dutch girl with inflatable shoes last week, phoned her up to arrange a date but unfortunately she'd popped her clogs

~~~~~~~~~~~~~~~~~~~~~~~~~~~~~~~~~~~~

So I said to the Gym instructor
"Can you teach me to do the splits?".
He said "How flexible are you?".
I said "I can't make Tuesdays"

Golf Cheats!?

Jeff and Ian were out for their usual round of golf one day. "Tell you what, Ian, let's make this game worth our time. I'll bet you a dollar that I score lower than you do this round."

"Sounds good, Jeff."

And they were off. They matched scores for the first eight holes, and things were looking good when they teed off on the ninth. After their first drives, they trooped off for the next stroke. Problem was, Jeff could not find his golf ball. He looked all over, but to no avail. "Ian, help me look for the ball!" "I'll look around from here, Jeff, but don't forget--a lost ball counts as four strokes!" Jeff looked around some more, but couldn't find the ball. Finally, out of desperation, he snuck a new ball out of his pocket, and dropped it on the ground when Ian was not looking. "Ian, I've found it!" he then yelled. Ian exploded: "You cheater! How dare you! I never thought that any man I played a friendly round with would stoop to cheating for a mere dollar!" Jeff replied, "What do you mean 'cheater'? I found that ball, I'll play it where it lies!" Ian said,

"That's not your golf ball! I've been standing on your ball for five minutes!"

~~~~~~~~~~~~~~~~~~~~~~~~~~~~~~

The bride came down the aisle and when she reached the altar, the groom was standing there with his golf bag and clubs by his side. She said, "What are your golf clubs doing here?" He looked her right in the eye--and said, "This isn't going to take all day, is it?"

The REAL Laws of Golf – 1

LAW 1: No matter how bad your last shot was, the worst is yet to come. This law does not expire on the 18th hole, since it has the supernatural tendency to extend over the course of a tournament, a summer and, eventually, a lifetime.

LAW 2: Your best round of golf will be followed almost immediately by your worst round ever. The probability of the latter increases with the number of people you tell about the former.

LAW 3: Brand new golf balls are water-magnetic. Though this cannot be proven in the lab, it is a known fact that the more expensive the golf ball, the greater its attraction to water.

LAW 4: Golf balls never bounce off of trees back into play. If one does, the tree is breaking a law of the universe and should be cut down.

LAW 5: No matter what causes a golfer to duff a shot, all his playing partners must solemnly chant "You looked up," or invoke the wrath of the universe.

LAW 6: The higher a golfer's handicap, the more qualified he deems himself as an instructor.

The REAL Laws of Golf – 2

LAW 7: Every par-three hole in the world has a secret desire to humiliate golfers. The shorter the hole, the greater its desire.

LAW 8: Topping a 3-iron is the most painful torture known to man.

LAW 9: Golf balls from the same "sleeve" tend to follow one another, particularly out of bounds or into the water (see Law three)

LAW 10: A severe slice is a thing of awesome power and beauty.

LAW 11: "Nice lag" can usually be translated to "lousy putt." Similarly, "tough break" can usually be translated "way to miss an easy one, sucker."

LAW 12: The person you would most hate to lose to will always be the one who beats you.

LAW 13: All vows taken on a golf course shall be valid only until the sunset of the same day.

SENIORS

One day three elderly Senior Golfers were having their weekly round when the 60 year old said "Well, life sure gets tough when you get on in years". His 70 year old companion asked what he meant. The younger man said "well, every day I wake up at 6:00 am and want a pee, however, no matter how I try it won't come, I run water, shake it, no way".

The 70 year old finished putting, thought and said " Man, you got it easy, every day I wake at 6:00 and want a poo. No matter how I grunt and strain, no luck, even medicine does not work".

Their older partner, an 80 year old who had been quietly listening advised.." Your both lucky, my problems are much worse. One of the men asked how come and he replied "Every day I pee at 6:00 and every day I poo at 6:05". His friends looked at him and ask "how can that be so bad".

Trees

The older man replied "I don't wake up until 6:30". A grandfather and grandson were playing golf together. On a severely dog-legged par 4, the grandfather told the grandson, "When I was your age, I'd aim right over those trees and hit the green every time." The grandson thought about that comment and decided to give it a try. He hit a perfect drive, but it landed right in the middle of the 50 ft trees.

The grandson looked sadly at the grandfather who said, "Of course when I was your age, those trees were 5 feet tall."

Saturday Morning at the Golf Club

It was a sunny Saturday morning on the first hole of a busy course and a guy was beginning his pre-shot routine, visualizing his upcoming effort when a piercing voice came over the clubhouse loud speaker.

"Would the gentleman on the woman's tee back up to the men's tee please!!"

Every eye on the course turned to look at him. He was still deep in his routine, seemingly impervious to the interruption.
Again the announcement,
"Would the MAN on the WOMAN'S tee kindly back up to the men's tee".

He again ignored the announcement and kept concentrating, when once more, the man yelled:
"WOULD THE MAN ON THE WOMAN'S TEE BACK UP TO THE MEN'S TEE, PLEASE!!!"

The golfer finally stopped, turned, looked through the clubhouse window directly at the person with the microphone, cupped his hands and shouted back........

"WOULD THE ASSHOLE IN THE CLUB HOUSE KINDLY SHUT THE FUCK UP AND LET ME PLAY MY SECOND SHOT!!!!!"

The hole-in-one!

A vicar, an avid though barely average golfer, woke early one Sunday to a clear, warm, beautiful morning. Just this once, he thought, "I'll give church a miss and play a round of golf."

So he loaded up his clubs and headed off alone to a golf course far enough away so he would be sure not to be recognized..

After a while the vicar was enjoying himself and feeling quite good about his decision to play. Just then an angel brought the vicar's Sunday morning activities to God's attention. God told the angel not to worry, that He would take care of the situation.

With the angel looking on God said, "Watch this." Just then the vicar teed off. The ball flew straight and true -- a hole in one! The vicar was ecstatic.

The angel protested, "I thought You said You were going to take care of the situation!" To which God replied, "I did......... Who can he tell?"

That's not fair

Moses and Jesus were playing golf.

Moses tees off and the ball goes in the water. Moses parts the water and chips onto the green. Jesus tee shot also goes in the water, but stays on top of the water and Jesus walks on the water and chips up on the green.

A third shot also lands in the water and a fish grabs it in its mouth. An eagle picks up the fish and drops it on the green, the ball rolls out of the fish's mouth and into the cup.

Moses says to Jesus, "I just hate playing with your Father".

You'll never hit her from here!

A guy stood over his tee shot for what seemed an eternity; looking up, looking down, measuring the distance, figuring the wind direction and speed. Driving his partner nuts. Finally his exasperated partner says, "What's taking so long? Hit the blasted ball!"

The guy answers, "My wife is up there watching me from the clubhouse. I want to make this a perfect shot."

"Forget it, man-you don't stand a snowball's chance in hell of hitting her from here!"

Now you tell me!!

A retiree was given a set of golf clubs by his co-workers. Thinking he'd try the game, he asked the local pro for lessons, explaining that he knew nothing whatever of the game.

The pro showed him the stance and swing, then said, "Just hit the ball toward the flag on the first green."

The novice teed up and smacked the ball straight down the fairway and onto the green, where it stopped inches from the hole. "Now what ?" the fellow asked the speechless pro.

"Uh... you're supposed to hit the ball into the cup." the pro finally said, after he was able to speak again.

"Oh great ! NOW you tell me." said the beginner.

It's the least I could do.

A man and his friend are playing golf one day at their local golf course. One of the men is about to chip onto the green when he sees a long funeral procession on the road next to the golf course. He stops in mid-swing, takes off his golf cap, closes his eyes, and bows his head down in prayer.

His friend says, "Wow, that is the most thoughtful and touching thing I have ever seen. You truly are a kind man."
The man shrugs then replies, "Yeah, well, I owe her that much, we were married for 35 years."

I'd Give Anything...........

A golfer is in a competitive match with a friend, who is ahead by a couple of strokes. The golfer says to himself: "I'd give anything to sink this next putt."

A stranger walks up to him and whispers: "Would you give up a fourth of your sex life?" The golfer thinks the man is crazy and that his answer will be meaningless but also that perhaps this is a good omen and will put him in the right frame of mind to make the difficult putt and says, "OK." And sinks the putt.

Two holes later he mumbles to himself: "Boy, if I could only get an eagle on this hole." The same stranger moves to his side and says, "Would it be worth another fourth of your sex life?" The golfer shrugs and says, "Sure." And he makes an eagle.

Down to the final hole. The golfer needs yet another eagle to win. Though he says nothing, the stranger moves to his side and says, "Would you be willing to give up the rest of your sex life to win this match?"

The golfer says, "Certainly." And makes the eagle. As the golfer walks to the club house, the stranger walks alongside and says, "You know, I've really not been fair with you because you don't know who I am. I'm the devil, and from now on you will have no sex life."

"Nice to meet you," says the golfer. "My name's Father O'Malley."

I Can't See Clearly Now....

"How was your golf game, dear?" asked Jack's wife Tracy.

"Well, I was hitting pretty well, but my eyesight's gotten so bad I couldn't see where the ball went."

"But you're seventy-five years old, Jack!" admonished his wife, "Why don't you take my brother Scott along?"

"But he's eighty-five, suffering with Alzheimer's and doesn't even play golf anymore," protested Jack.

"But he's got perfect eyesight. He could watch your ball," Tracy pointed out.

The next day Jack teed off with Scott looking on. Jack swung, and the ball disappeared down the middle of the fairway. "Do you see it?" asked Jack.

"Yup," Scott answered.

They walked 200 yards down the fairway.

"Well, where is it?" yelled Jack, peering off into the distance.

"Where's what?" Said Scott

~~~~~~~~~~~~~~~~~~~~~~~~~~~~~~~

GREEN SIDE UP!

A foursome of senior golfers hit the course with waning enthusiasm for the sport.

"These hills are getting steeper as the years go by," one complained.

"These fairways seem to be getting longer too," said one of the others.

"The sand traps seem to be bigger than I remember them too," said the third senior.

After hearing enough from his Senior buddies, the oldest, and the wisest of the four of them at 87 years old, piped up and said, "Oh my friends, just be thankful we're still on this side of the grass!"

Pebble Beach

A golfer who was well into his golden years had a lifelong ambition to play one hole at Pebble Beach, California, the way the pros do it. The pros drive the ball out over the water onto the green that is on a spit of land that just out off the coast. It was something he had tried hundreds of times without success. His ball always fell short, into the water. Because of this he never used a new ball on this particular hole. He always picked out one that had a cut or a nick.

One year he went out to Pebble Beach to try again. When he came to the fateful hole, he teed up an old cut ball and said a silent prayer. Before he hit it, however, a powerful voice from above said WAIT ... REPLACE THAT OLD BALL WITH A BRAND-NEW BALL. He complied, with some slight misgiving, despite the fact that the Lord seemed to be implying that HE was going to let him finally achieve his lifelong ambition. As he stepped up to the tee once more, the voice came down again WAIT .. STEP BACK ... TAKE A PRACTICE SWING. So he stepped back and took a practice swing. The voice boomed out again TAKE ANOTHER PRACTICE SWING. He did.

Silence followed. Then the voice spoke out again

WAIT.....PUT THE OLD BALL BACK.

A Coincidence

After a long day on the course, the exasperated golfer turned to his caddy and said, "You must be the absolute worst caddy in the world." "No, I don't think so," said the caddy. "That would be too much of a coincidence."

New Clubs

A golfer who was known for his bad temper walked into the pro shop one day and plunked down big bucks for a new set of woods. The staff all watched to see what would happen after he used them for the first time - more than half expecting he'd come in and demand his money back.   But the next time he came in, he was all smiles.

"They're the best clubs I've ever had," he said. "In fact, I've discovered I can throw them at least 40 yards farther than I could my last ones."

Wow, that's Great

Caddy: Sir, you've just aced the eighteenth hole.

Golfer: Wow! That's great!

Caddy: Not really. We're on the fourteenth hole.

Slow golfers ahead of us

Joe decides to take his boss Phil to play 9 holes on their lunch. While both men are playing excellent golf, two women in front of them often hold them up, moving at a very slow pace. Joe offers to talk to the women and see if they can speed it up a bit. He gets about half of the way there stops and jogs back.

His boss asks what the problem is. "Well one of those women is my wife and the other my mistress," complained Joe. Phil just shook his head at Joe and started toward the women determined to finish his round of golf. Preparing to ask the ladies to speed up their game, he too stopped short and turned around.

Joe asked "what's wrong?" It's a small, small world Joe, and you're fired"

Put or Putt?

A woman was taking her first golf lesson. "Is the word spelled 'put' or 'putt'?" she asked the instructor.

"'Putt' is correct," he replied. "'Put' means to place a thing where you want it. 'Putt' means a vain attempt to do the same thing."

Ten Years On A Deserted Island

A man is stranded on a desert island, all alone for ten years. One day, he sees a speck in the horizon. He thinks to himself, "It's not a ship." The speck gets a little closer and he thinks, "It's not a boat." The speck gets even closer and he thinks, "It's not a raft." Then, out of the surf comes this gorgeous blonde woman, wearing a wet suit and scuba gear. She comes up to the guy and says, "How long has it been since you've had a cigarette?"

"Ten years!", he says.

She reaches over and unzips a waterproof pocket on her left sleeve and pulls out a pack of fresh cigarettes.

He takes one, lights it, takes a long drag, and says, "Man, oh man! Is that good!"

Then she asked, "How long has it been since you've had a drink of whiskey?"

He replies, "Ten years!"

She reaches over, unzips her waterproof pocket on her right sleeve, pulls out a flask and gives it to him.

He takes a long swig and says, "Wow, that's fantastic!"

Then she starts unzipping a longer zipper that runs down the front of her wet suit and she says to him, "And how long has it been since you've had some real fun?"

And the man replies, "Wow! Don't tell me that you've got golf clubs in there!"

IT MAKES THE DAY GO ROUND.....

"Squawks" are problems noted by U.S. Air Force pilots and left for maintenance crews to fix before the next flight. Here are some actual maintenance complaints logged by those Air Force pilots and the replies from the maintenance crews.
(P) = Problem
(S) = Solution

(P) Left inside main tyre almost needs replacement.
(S) Almost replaced left inside main tyre.

(P) Test flight OK, except auto land very rough.
(S) Auto land not installed on this aircraft.

(P) a 2 propeller seeping prop fluid.
(S) a 2 propeller seepage normal - a 1, a 3, and a 4 propellers lack normal seepage.

(P) Something loose in cockpit.
(S) Something tightened in cockpit.

(P) Evidence of leak on right main landing gear.
(S) Evidence removed.

(P) DME volume unbelievably loud.
(S) Volume set to more believable level.

(P) Dead bugs on windshield.
(S) Live bugs on order.

(P) Autopilot in altitude hold mode produces a 200 fpm descent.
(S) Cannot reproduce problems on ground.

(P) IFF inoperative.
(S) IFF always inoperative in OFF mode.

(P) Friction locks cause throttle levers to stick.
(S) That's what they're there for.

(P) Number three engine missing.
(S) Engine found on right wing after brief search.

(P) Aircraft handles funny.
(S) Aircraft warned to straighten up, "fly right," and be serious.

(P) Target Radar hums.
(S) Target Radar reprogrammed with the words.

The Seven dwarfs were in a sauna feeling happy.
So Happy got up and left.

Doctor Dave

Doctor Dave had slept with one of his patients and felt guilty all day long. No matter how much he tried to forget about it, he couldn't. The guilt and sense of betrayal was overwhelming. But every once in a while he'd hear an internal, reassuring voice that said:

"Dave, don't worry about it. You aren't the first doctor to sleep with one of their patients and you won't be the last. And you're single anyway.

Just let it go..."

But invariably the other voice would bring him back to reality, whispering:

"Dave, you're a vet..."

IN THE GARDEN OF EDEN

One day in the Garden of Eden, Eve calls out to God... "Lord, I have a problem."

"What's the problem, Eve?"
"I know that you created me and provided this beautiful garden and all of these wonderful animals, as well as that hilarious comedic snake, but I'm just not happy."
"And why is that Eve?"
"Lord, I am lonely, and I'm sick to death of apples."
"Well, Eve, in that case, I have a solution. I shall create a man for you."
"Man? What is that Lord?"

"A flawed creature, with many bad traits. He'll lie, cheat and be vain; all in all, he'll give you a hard time. But he'll be bigger, faster and will like to hunt and kill things. He will look silly when he is aroused, but since you've been complaining, I'll create him in such a way that he will satisfy your physical needs. He will be witless and will revel in childish things like fighting and kicking a ball about. He won't be too smart, so he will also need your advice to think properly."
"Sounds great," says Eve, with ironically raised eyebrows, "but what's the catch, Lord?"
"Well... you can have him on one condition."
"And what's that Lord?"
"As I said, he'll be proud, arrogant and self-admiring... so you'll have to let him believe that I made him first. And it will have to be our little secret.

You know, woman to woman."

Americans – the wrong decision again?.......

The only seat available on the train from London to Paris
was directly adjacent to a well-dressed middle-aged French woman,
and her dog was using the seat.

The weary traveller asked, "Ma'am, please move your dog. I need
that seat."

The French woman looked down her nose at the American, sniffed
and said, "You Americans. You are such a rude class of people. Can't
you see my little Fifi is using that seat?

The American walked away, determined to find a place to rest, but
after another trip down to the end of the train, found himself again
facing the woman with the dog. Again he asked, "Please, lady. May I sit
there? I'm very tired." The French woman wrinkled her nose and
snorted, "You Americans! Not only are you rude, you are also
arrogant.

The American didn't say anything else. He leaned over, picked up the
dog, tossed it out the window of the train and sat down in the
empty seat. The woman shrieked and wailed, demanding that
someone defend her honour and chastise the American.

An English man sitting across the aisle spoke up indignantly, "You
know, sir, you Americans do seem to have a history for doing the
wrong thing. You eat holding the fork in the wrong hand. You drive
your cars on the wrong side of the road, and now you've thrown the
wrong bitch out the window."

TV GAFFS!

Chris Tarrant discussing the first Millionaire winner Judith Keppel on "This Morning" programme:
"She was practising fastest finger first by herself in bed last night."

Claire Frisby talking about a jumbo hot dog on **"Look North"** said:
"There's nothing like a big hot sausage inside you on a cold night like this."

WINNING Post's Stewart Machin commentating on jockey Tony McCoy's
formidable lead in the race:
"Tony has a quick look between his legs and likes what he sees."

ROSS King discussing relays with champion runner Phil Redmond:
"Well Phil, tell us about your amazing third leg."

Good Vibrations

As a woman passed her daughter's closed bedroom door, she heard a strange buzzing noise coming from within.
Opening the door, she observed her daughter giving herself a real workout with a vibrator.
Shocked, she asked, "what in the world are you doing?"

The daughter replied, "Mom, I'm thirty-five years old, unmarried, and this is about as close as I'll ever get to a husband. Please, go away and leave me alone."

The next day, the girl's father heard the same buzz coming from the other side of the closed bedroom door. Upon entering the room, he observed his daughter making passionate love to her vibrator.
To his query as to what she was doing, the daughter said, "Dad, I'm thirty five years old, unmarried, and this thing is about as close as I'll ever get to a husband.
Please, go away and leave me alone."

A couple days later, the wife came home from a shopping trip, placed the groceries on the kitchen counter, and heard that buzzing noise coming from, of all places, the family room.
She entered that area and observed her husband sitting on the couch, staring at the TV.
The vibrator was next to him on the couch, buzzing like crazy.

The wife asked in a demanding tone, "What the hell are you doing?"
The husband replied: "I'm watching the football game with my son-in-law."

The London Underground System!

The London Underground system is used by some 20 million people per day, and generally works well. However, there are obviously times when drivers become frustrated and use their tannoy system to vent their feelings to the passengers!

These are some excerpts reported by passengers to an Underground Website........

Please allow the doors to close. Try not to confuse this with 'Please hold the doors open.' The two are distinct and separate instructions."

"Please note that the beeping noise coming from the doors means that the doors are about to close. It does not mean throw yourself or your bags into the doors."

"Ladies and Gentlemen, I do apologise for the delay to your service. I know you're all dying to get home unless, of course, you happen to be married to my ex-wife, in which case you'll want to cross over to the westbound platform and go in the opposite direction.

"I am sorry about the delay, apparently some nutter has just wandered into the tunnel at Euston. We don't know when we'll be moving again, but these people tend to come out pretty quickly... usually in bits."

"Your delay this evening is caused by the line controller suffering from elbow and backside syndrome, that is not knowing one from the other.
I'll let you know any further information as soon as I'm given any".

"Ladies and Gentlemen, last Friday was my birthday and I hit the town and had a great time. But I felt sadly let down by the fact that none of you sent me a card! I drive you to work and home each day and not even a card."

Nowadays 80% of women are against marriage, as they have wisened up to the fact that for 200 grams of sausage it's not worth buying the entire pig !!!!

There's nothing like a good curry.....

An Englishman, Welshman, Scotsman and an Irishman were all sitting down discussing what is the fastest thing in life.
After much deliberation the Englishman said,

"I believe it is the process of thought, it comes out in a flash"

"Good try" agreed the Scot, "but I think "blinking" is even quicker."

"Pretty good but not quick enough, " quipped the Welshman. "I am sure electricity is faster; just think if you hit any light switch you get instant light"

After a few moments Paddy cut in, "I believe you all have valid points but I think Diarrhoea wins outroight!"

"What the hell are you talking about, Paddy?" chimed the three other guys.

"Well it is like this. Last night I went down to the local curry house for a vindaloo, which I washed down with 12 pints of Guinness, I then retired to bed.

However at 3 o'clock this morning, before I could think, blink or turn the light on, I shat myself!!

HELL? – Not Such A Bad Place After All

One day a guy died and found himself in hell. As he was wallowing in despair, he had his first meeting with a demon.

The demon asked, "Why so glum?"

The guy responded, "What do you think? I'm in hell!"

"Hell's not so bad," the demon said. "We actually have a lot of fun down here. You a drinking man?"

"Sure," the man said, "I love to drink."

"Well you're gonna love Mondays then. On Mondays all we do is drink. Whisky, Tequila, Guinness, wine coolers, diet Tab and Fresca. We drink till we throw up and then we drink some more!"

The guy is astounded. "Damn, that sounds great."

"You a smoker?" the demon asked. "You better believe it!"

"You're gonna love Tuesdays. We get the finest cigars from all over the world and smoke our lungs out. If you get cancer, no biggie. You're already dead, remember?" "Wow, the guy said, "that's awesome!"

The demon continued. "I bet you like to gamble."

"Why yes, as a matter of fact I do."

"Wednesdays you can gamble all you want. Blackjack, roulette, poker, slots, whatever. If you go bankrupt, well, you're dead anyhow.

You into drugs?" The guy said, "Are you kidding? I love drugs! You don't mean ..."

"That's right! Thursday is drug day. Help yourself to a great big bowl of crack, or smack. Smoke a doobie the size of a submarine. You can do all the drugs you want, you're dead, who cares!"

"Wow," the guy said, starting to feel better about his situation, "I never realized Hell was such a cool place!"

The demon said, "You gay?"

"No." "Aaaahh, you won't be too keen on Fridays then!"

Captain Hook

A pirate walks into a bar and the bartender says, "Hey, I haven't seen you in a while. What happened, you look terrible!"

"What do you mean?" the pirate replies, "I'm fine."

The bartender says, "But what about that wooden leg? You didn't have that before."

"Well," says the pirate, "We were in a battle at sea and a cannon ball hit my leg but the surgeon fixed me up, and I'm fine, really."

"Yeah," says the bartender, "But what about that hook? Last time I saw you, you had both hands."

"Well," says the pirate, "We were in another battle and we boarded the enemy ship. I was in a sword fight and my hand was cut off but the surgeon fixed me up with this hook, and I feel great, really."

"Oh," says the bartender, "What about that eye patch? Last time you were in here you had both eyes."

"Well," says the pirate, "One day when we were at sea, some birds were flying over the ship. I looked up, and one of them shat in my eye."

"So?" replied the bartender, "what happened? You couldn't have lost an eye just from some bird shit!"

"Ahh," says the pirate, "I really hadn't got used to the hook at that time."

HOW TO SATISFY YOUR WOMAN

Three guys were sitting in a bar talking. One was a Doctor, one was a Lawyer, and one was a Biker.

After a sip of his martini, the doctor said;
"You know, tomorrow is my anniversary. I got my wife a diamond ring and a new Mercedes. I figure that if she doesn't like the diamond ring, she will at least like the Mercedes, and she will know that I love her.

After finishing his scotch, the lawyer replied; "Well, on my last anniversary, I got my wife a string of pearls and a trip to the Bahamas. Figured if she didn't like the pearls, she would at least like the trip, and she would know that I love her."

The Biker then took a big swig from his beer, and said; "Ah, well for my anniversary, I got my old lady a tee-shirt and a vibrator. I figured if she didn't like the tee shirt, she can go fuck herself."

Perfect Fit

A man walks into doctor's office. "What seems to be the problem?" asks the doc. "It's... um... well... I have five penises." replies the man "Blimey!" says the doctor, "How do your trousers fit?"
"Like a glove."

A BEAUTIFUL VALENTINES DAY STORY

I was happy. My girlfriend and I were dating for over a year, and so we decided to get married. My parents helped us in every way, my friends encouraged me, and my girlfriend? She was a dream!
There was only one thing bothering me, and that was my mother-in-law to be. She was a career woman, smart, but most of all beautiful and sexy, who sometimes flirted with me, which made me feel uncomfortable.
One day she called me and asked me to come over to check the wedding invitations. So I went. She was alone, and when I arrived, she whispered to me, that soon I was to be married, and she had feelings and desires for me that she couldn't overcome. So before I got married and committed my life to her daughter, she wanted to make love to me just once...
What could I say? I was in total shock, and couldn't say a word.
So, she said, I'll go to the bedroom, and if you are up for it, just come and get me.
I just watched her as she went up the stairs.
I stood there for a moment, and then turned around and went to the front door...
I opened it, and stepped out of the house.
Her husband and my girlfriend were standing outside, and with tears in their eyes, they both hugged me and said, we are very happy and pleased, you have passed our little test.
We couldn't have asked for a better man for our daughter.
Welcome to the family.

Moral of the story?............................

"Always keep your condoms in the car."

Spaghetti?

A wealthy man was having an affair with an Italian woman for several years. One night, during one of their rendezvous, she confided in him that she was pregnant. Not wanting to ruin his reputation or his marriage, he paid her a large sum of money if she would go to Italy to secretly have the child. If she stayed in Italy to raise the child, he would also provide child support until the child turned 18. She agreed, but asked how he would know when the baby was born. To keep it discrete, he told her to simply mail him a post card, and write "Spaghetti" on the back. He would then arrange for child support payments to begin. One day, about 9 months later, he came home to his confused wife. Honey," she said, "you received a very strange post card today." "Oh, just give it to me and I'll explain it later," he said. The wife obeyed and watched as her husband read the card, turned white and fainted!

On the card was written:
"Spaghetti, Spaghetti, Spaghetti.
Two with meatballs,
One without."

Facelift

A man decides to have a face-lift for his birthday. He spends £5,000 and feels really good about the result.

On his way home he pops into the newsagent and buys a paper. Before leaving he says to the newsagent "I hope you don't mind me asking, but how old do you think I am?"

"About 35" was the reply.

"I'm actually 47 years old" the man says, feeling really happy.

After that he goes into the Fish & Chip shop to celebrate. Before leaving, he asks the same question, to which the reply is "Oh, you look about 29" This makes him feel really good.

Whilst standing at the bus stop he asks an old woman the same question.

She replies, "I am 85 years old and my eyesight is going. But when I was young there was a sure way of telling a mans age. If I put my hand down your trousers and play with your balls for ten minutes I will be able to tell your exact age."

Being as there was nobody around the man thought what the hell and let her slip her hand down his trousers.

Ten minutes later the old lady says "You are 47 years old."

Stunned the man says, "That was brilliant. How did you do that?"

The old lady replies, "I was behind you in the paper shop!"

ESSEX Girls – love'em!

An Essex Girl enters a sex shop & asks for a vibrator.
The man says "Choose from our range on the wall."
She says "I'll take the red one."
The man replies "That's a fire extinguisher." .

~~~~~~~~~~~~~~~~~~~~~~~~~~~~~~~~~

An Essex girl is involved in a nasty car crash and is trapped and bleeding. The paramedics soon arrive on site.

Medic: It's OK I'm a paramedic and I'm going to ask you some questions?
Girl: OK.
Medic: What's your name?
Girl: Sharon.
Medic: OK Sharon, is this your car?
Sharon: Yes.
Medic: Where are you bleeding from?
Sharon: Romford mate.

~~~~~~~~~~~~~~~~~~~~~~~~~~~~~~~

An Essex girl was driving down the A13 when her car phone rang. It was her boyfriend, urgently warning her,
"Treacle, I just heard on the news that there's a car going the wrong way on the A13. Please be careful."
"It's not just one car." said the Essex girl,
"There's hundreds of them!"

It is good to be a woman because......

1. We got off the Titanic first.

2. We can scare male bosses with the mysterious gynaecological disorder excuses.

3. Taxis stop for us.

4. We don't look like a frog in a blender when dancing.

5. No fashion faux pas we make could ever rival the Speedo.

6. We don't have to pass gas to amuse ourselves.

7. If we forget to shave, no one has to know.

8. We can congratulate our team-mate without ever touching her rear end.

9. We never have to reach down every so often to make sure our privates are still there.

10. We have the ability to dress ourselves.

11. We can talk to the opposite sex without having to picture them naked.

12. If we marry someone 20 years younger, we are aware that we will look like an idiot.

13. We will never regret piercing our ears.

14. There are times when chocolate really can solve all your problems.

15. We can make comments about how silly men are in their presence because they aren't listening anyway.

What Goes Around, Comes Around… Again!

At age 4   .... success is .... not peeing in your pants.

At age 12 .... success is .... having friends.

At age 17 .... success is .... having a drivers license.

At age 20 .... success is .... having sex.

At age 35 .... success is .... having money.

At age 50 .... success is .... having money.

At age 60 .... success is .... having sex.

At age 70 .... success is .... having a drivers license.

At age 75 .... success is .... having friends.

At age 80 .... success is .... not peeing in your pants.

TV GAFFS!

Cricketer Neil Fairbrother hit a single during a Durham v Lancashire match, inspiring Bobby Simpson to observe: "With his lovely soft hands he just tossed it off."

Michael Buerk watching Phillipa Forrester cuddle up to a male astronomer for warmth during BBC1's UK eclipse coverage remarked:
"They seem cold out there, they're rubbing each other and he's only come in his shorts."

Ken Brown commentating on golfer Nick Faldo and his caddie Fanny Sunneson lining-up shots at the Scottish Open: "Some weeks Nick likes to use Fanny, other weeks he prefers to do it by himself."

Mike Hallett discussing missed snooker shots on Sky Sports:
"Stephen Hendry jumps on Steve Davis's misses every chance he gets."

Jack Burnicle was talking about Colin Edwards' tyre choice on World Superbike racing: "Colin had a hard on in practice earlier, and I bet he wished he had a hard on now."

Directory Enquiries (pre 118)

The following are real conversations Directory Enquiries operators had with callers, as revealed in interviews with staff at the Cardiff Directory Enquires Centre.

C= Caller and O = Operator.
****

C: I'd like the number of the Argoed Fish Bar in Cardiff, please.
O: I'm sorry, there's no listing. Is the spelling correct?
C: Well, it used to be called the Bargoed Fish Bar but the B fell off.

C: I'd like the number of the Scottish knitwear company in Woven.
O: I can't find a town called 'Woven'? Are you sure?
C: Yes. That's what it says on the label - Woven in Scotland.

C: I'd like the RSPCA please.
O: Where are you calling from?
C: The living room

C: The water board please.
O: Which department?
C: Tap water

O: How are you spelling that?
C: With letters.

C: I'd like the number for a reverend in Cardiff, please.
O: Do you have his name?
C: No, but he has a dog named Ben.

C: The Union of Shopkeepers and Alligators please.
O: You mean the Amalgamated Union of Shopkeepers?
C: Er, yes.

A Wonderfully True Poem

When I was in my younger days, I weighed a few pounds less

I needn't hold my tummy in to wear a belted dress.

But now that I am older, I've set my body free;

There's comfort of elastic, where once my waist would be.

Inventor of those high-heeled shoes, my feet have not forgiven;

I have to wear a nine now, but used to wear a seven.

And how about those pantyhose, they're sized by weight, you see,

So how come when I put them on, the crotch is at my knee?

I need to wear these glasses, as the print's been getting smaller;

And it wasn't very long ago, I know that I was taller.

Though my hair has turned to grey, and my skin no longer fits,

On the inside, I'm the same old me, it's the outside's changed a bit.

by Maya Angelou

A woman's prayer

Lord:
Before I lay myself down to sleep,
I pray for a man, who's not a creep,
One who's handsome, smart and strong,
One who's willy's strong, thick and long.
One who thinks before he speaks,
When promises to call, he won't wait weeks.

I pray that he is gainfully employed,
And when I spend his cash, wont be annoyed.
Pulls out my chair and opens my door,
Massages my back and begs to do more.

Oh! send me a man who will make love to my mind,
Knows just what to say, when I ask "How big's my behind?"
One who'll make love till my body is twitchin,
In the hall, in the loo, in the garden and in the kitchen!

I pray that this man will love me no end,
And never attempts to shag my best friend.
But as I kneel and pray by my bed,
I look at the w@nker you sent me instead.

A Man's Prayer:

Lord
I pray for a lady with big tits.

Amen

Essex Girls

Two Essex girls walk up to a perfume counter in the department store and pick up a sample bottle, Sharon sprays it on her wrist and smells it, "That's quite nice innit, don't you fink Trace?", "Yeah, what's it called?", "Viens a moi",
"VIENS A MOI, what the f**k does that mean?"

At this stage the assistant offers some help.

PUB CLASSIC

"Viens a moi, ladies is French for 'come to me'"

Sharon takes another sniff and offers her arm to Tracey again, saying, "That doesn't smell like come to me Trace.
Does it smell like come to you?"

~~~~~~

Classic Bumper Sticker

The More you Complain – The Longer God Lets You Live!

The Postman Always Knocks Twice?

A man was in his front yard mowing grass when his attractive blond female neighbour came out of the house and went straight to the mailbox.

She opened it then slammed it shut and stormed back in the house. A little later she came out of her house again went to the mailbox and again opened it, slammed it shut again.

Angrily, back into the house she went.

As the man was getting ready to edge the lawn, here she came out again, marched to the mailbox, opened it and then slammed it closed harder than ever.

Puzzled by her actions the man asked her, "Is something wrong?"

To which she replied, "There certainly is!"

"My stupid computer keeps saying:

You've Got Mail

LET ME BUY YOU A DRINK!

1st Man: Oh hello, how are you, let me buy you a drink!

2nd Man: Why thank you." he replies. "Where are you from?

1st Man: Oh, I'm from Ireland," he replies.

2nd Man: You don't say. I'm from Ireland too! Let's have another round to Ireland.

1st Man: Of course!

And they both knock back their drinks....

2nd Man: So, where in Ireland are you from?

1st Man: Dublin," comes the reply.

2nd Man: I can't believe it says the first man. I'm from Dublin too! Let's have another drink to Dublin!

1st Man: Aye! why not!" And both men continue drinking.

2nd Man: So, like... hmmmm... What school did you go to?

1st Man: St. Mary's, I graduated in '62.

2nd Man: You don't say! This is bloody unbelievable, I went to St. Mary's and I graduated in '62, too!

1st Man: Noooo way???

About that time, in comes one of the regulars and sits down at the bar. "What's been going on?" he asks the bartender. "Oh nothing much," replies the bartender. "The O'Malley twins are drunk again."

THREE LITTLE PIGS
(One for the kids' bedtime story...)

Three Little Pigs went out to dinner one night. The waiter comes and takes their drink order.

"I would like a Sprite," said the first little piggy.
"I would like a Coke," said the second little piggy.
"I want water, lots and lots of water," said the third little piggy.

The drinks are brought out and the waiter takes their orders for dinner.

"I want a nice big steak," said the first piggy.
"I would like the salad plate," said the second piggy.
"I want water, lots and lots of water," said the third little piggy.

The meals were brought out and a while later the waiter approached the table and asked if the piggies would like any dessert.

"I want a banana split," said the first piggy.
"I want a root beer float," said the second piggy.
"I want water, lots and lots of water," exclaimed the third little piggy.

"Pardon me for asking," said the waiter! to the third little piggy, "but why have you only ordered water all evening?"

The third piggy says -

"Well, somebody has to go 'Wee, wee, wee, all the way home!"

CODE FOR SEX

A newly married couple returned to their house after being on honeymoon.
'Care to go upstairs and have a shag?' the husband asks.
'Shhh!' said the bride. 'All the neighbours will know what we're about to do. These walls are paper-thin. In the future, we'll have to ask each other in code. For example, how about asking,
"Have you left the washing machine door open" instead?'
So the following night, the husband asks, 'I don't suppose you left the washing machine door open did you?'
'No, I definitely shut it,' replied the wife who rolled over and went to sleep.
When she woke up, however, she was feeling a little randy herself and she nudged her husband and said, 'I think I did leave the washing machine door open after all. Would you like to do some washing?'
'No thanks,' said the husband, 'it was only a small load and I've done it by hand.'

The Important Women In Your Life

1. It is important that a woman does all (most) of the housework
2. It is important that a woman makes you laugh.
3. It is important to find a woman you can count on and does not lie to you.
4. It is important that a woman is good in bed.

5. It is really important that these four women don't know each other.

INDIAN PROVERB

Onestone was his name...........

This was his Indian name because he had only one testicle.
After years and years of this torment Onestone cracked and said, "If
anyone calls me Onestone again I will kill them!"

The word got around and nobody called him Onestone any more.
Then one day a young girl forgot and said, "Good morning
Onestone." He jumped up, grabbed her and took her deep into the
forest, there he shagged her all day, he shagged her all night, he
shagged her all the next day, until she died from exhaustion. The
word got around that Onestone meant business.

Many peaceful years passed until a woman returned to the village
after many years away.

She was overjoyed when she saw Onestone and hugged him and
said," Good to see you Onestone." Again, Onestone grabbed her
and took her deep into the forest where he shagged her all day,
shagged her all night, shagged her all the next day, shagged her all the
next night, but she wouldn't die!

What is the moral of the story?

You can't kill two birds with one stone!!!!!

WHO SHOULD BE IN CHARGE?

"I should be in charge" said the blood, "because I circulate oxygen

all over so without me you'd all waste away."

 "I should be in charge, " said the stomach,

" because I process food and give all of you energy."

"I should be in charge" said the legs,

"because I carry the body wherever it needs to go."

"I should be in charge" said the eyes,

"because I allow the body to see where it goes."

"I should be in charge, "said the rectum,

"Because I'm responsible for waste removal."

All the other body parts laughed at the rectum and insulted him,

so in a huff, he shut down tight.

Within a few days, the brain had a terrible headache, the stomach
was bloated, the legs got wobbly, the eyes got watery, and the blood
was toxic.

They all decided that the rectum should be the boss.

The Moral of the story is...

 In all walks of life it is usually the asshole that's in charge!

Wanna Hear A Blonde Joke from A Blind Man?

A blind man enters a lesbian bar by mistake. He finds his way to a stool and orders a drink. After sitting there for a while, he yells to the
bartender, "Hey, you wanna hear a blonde joke?" The bar immediately falls absolutely quiet. In a very deep, husky voice the woman next to him says,

"Before you tell that joke, sir, you should know five things....

1. The bartender is a blonde girl.
2. The bouncer is a blonde girl.
3. I'm a 6 foot, 200-pound blonde woman with a black belt in karate.
4. The woman sitting on my left is blonde and is a professional weight
lifter.
5. The lady to your right is a blonde and is a professional wrestler.

Now think about it seriously, Mister. Do you still wanna tell that joke?"

The blind man thinks for a second, shakes his head, and "Nah, not if I'm gonna have to explain it five times."

Have you ever wondered..........

...why they don't make the whole plane out of the material used for the indestructible black box ?

Female Curiosity

Recently a "Husband Shopping Centre" opened in Dallas, where women could go to choose a husband from among many men. It was laid out in five floors, with the men increasing in positive attributes as you ascended.

The only rule was, once you opened the door to any floor, you HAD to choose a man from that floor; If you went up a floor, you couldn't go back down except to leave the place, never to return.

A couple of girlfriends went to the shopping centre to find some husbands...

First floor

The door had a sign saying, "These men have jobs and love kids.

The women read the sign and said, "Well, that's better than not having a job, or not loving kids, but I wonder what's further up?"

So up they went.

Second floor

The sign read, "These men have high paying jobs, love kids, and are extremely good looking." Hmmm, said the ladies. But, I wonder what's further up?

Third floor

This sign read, "These men have high paying jobs, are extremely good looking, love kids and help with the housework." Wow! said the women. Very tempting, BUT, there's more further up!

And up they went.

Fourth floor

This door had a sign saying "These men have high paying jobs, love kids, are extremely good looking, help with the housework, and have a strong romantic streak."

Oh, mercy me. But just think! what must be awaiting us further on!

So up to the fifth floor they went.

Fifth floor

The sign on that door said,

"This floor is empty and exists only to prove that women are f*cking impossible to please!".

At some distant point (hopefully), we may end up in a Retirement home.
The following scenario's can be looked forward to then... ...

1. "I CAN HEAR JUST FINE!"

Three retirees, each with a hearing loss, were playing golf one fine March
day. One remarked to the other, "Windy, isn't it?"
"No," the second man replied, "it's Thursday."
And the third man chimed in, "So am I. Let's have a beer."

---

2. SENIOR MOMENTS II

Two elderly ladies had been friends for many decades. Over the years they
had shared all kinds of activities and adventures.
Lately, their activities had been limited to meeting a few times a week to
play cards. One day they were playing cards when one looked at the other
and said, "Now don't get mad at me.....I know we've been friends for a long
time....but I just can't think of your name! I've thought and thought, but I
can't remember it. Please tell me what your name is."
Her friend glared at her. For at least three minutes she just stared
and glared at her. Finally she said, "How soon do you need to know?"

3. DOWN AT THE RETIREMENT CENTRE

80-year old Bessie bursts into the recreation room at the retirement home.
She holds her clenched fist in the air and announces, "Anyone who can
guess what's in my hand can have sex with me tonight!!"
An elderly gentleman in the rear shouts out, "An elephant?"
Bessie thinks a minute and says, "Close enough."

4. SENILE

Three sisters, ages 92, 94, and 96 live in a house together. One night the 96 year old draws a bath. She puts one foot in and pauses. She yells down the stairs,
"Was I getting in or out of the bath?"
The 94-year-old yells back, "I don't know. I'll come up and see."
She starts up the stairs and pauses. Then, she yells, "Was I going up the stairs or down?"
The 92 year old is sitting at the kitchen table having tea, listening to her sisters. She shakes her head and says, "I sure hope I never get that forgetful." She knocks on wood for good measure.
She then yells, "I'll come up and help both of you as soon as I see who's at the door."

---

5. DOWN AT THE NURSING HOME

A little old lady was running up and down the halls in a nursing home. As she walked, she would flip up the hem of her nightgown and say "supersex."

She walked up to an elderly man in a wheelchair. Flipping her gown at him, she said, "supersex."

He sat silently for a moment or two and finally answered, "I'll take the soup."

Women's Ass Size Study

There is a new study out about women and how they feel about their ass. The results were interesting.

85% of women think their ass is too big

10% of women think their ass is too little

The other 5% say that they don't care - they love him and would have

married him anyway

Chinese Sex Therapist

A woman was very distraught at the fact that she had not had a date or any sex in quite some time. She was afraid she might have something wrong with her, so she decided to seek the medical expertise of a sex therapist. Her doctor recommended that she see a well-known Chinese sex therapist, Dr. Chang. Upon entering the examination room, Dr. Chang said, "OK, take off all you crose."
The woman did as she was told.
"Now, get down and craw reery, reery fass to odder side of room."
Again, the woman did as she was instructed.
Dr. Chang then said, "OK, now craw reery, reery fass back to me."
So she did.
Dr. Chang shook his head slowly and said, "Your plobrem vewy bad.
You haf Ed Zachary Disease.
Worse case I ever see. Dat why you not haf sex or dates."
Worried, the woman asked anxiously, "Oh my God, Dr.Chang, what is Ed Zachary Disease?"

He replied: "Ed Zachary Disease is when your face rook Ed Zachary rike your arssse."

SEX IN THE DARK

There was this couple that had been married for 20 years. Every time they made love, the husband always insisted on shutting off the lights.

Well, after 20 years the wife felt this was ridiculous. She figured she would break him of this crazy habit. So one night, while they were in
the middle of a wild, screaming, romantic session, she turned on the lights.

She looked down .... and saw her husband was holding a battery operated pleasure device.. a vibrator ... soft, wonderful and larger than a real one. She goes completely ballistic.

"You impotent fake," she screamed at him, "how could you be lying to me all of these years? You better explain yourself!" ...

The husband looks her straight in the eyes and says calmly: "I'll explain the toy .... if you explain the kids."

Change is Inevitable – except from a vending machine

CIDER

A little girl came running into the house bawling her eyes out and cradling her hand: "Mummy, quick! Get me a glass of cider!" she wailed. "Why do you want a glass of cider?" asked her mom. "I cut my hand on a thorn, and I want the pain to go away!" Confused, but weary of the child's whining, the mother obliged and poured her a glass of cider. The little girl immediately dunked her hand in it. "Ouch! It still hurts! This cider doesn't work!" she whined. "What are you talking about?" asked her increasingly perplexed parent, "What ever made you think that cider would ease your pain?" "Well, I overheard my big sister say that whenever she gets a prick in her hand, she can't wait to get it in cider"

Have you ever wondered..........

...why the man who invests all your money is called a broker?

...why "abbreviated" is such a long word?

CUBICLE CHAT

This bloke walks into a public toilet in Sydney where he finds two cubicles; one is already occupied.

So he enters the other one, closes the door, drops'em and sits down.

A voice then comes from the cubicle next to him "G'day mate, how are you going?"

Thinking this a bit strange but not wanting to be rude the guy replies "Yeh, not too bad thanks"

After a short pause, he hears the voice again. "So, what are you up to mate?

Again answering reluctantly, but unsure what to say, replies, "Ahh, just having a quick crap. How about yourself?"

He then hears the voice for the 3rd time.....

"Sorry mate, I'll have to call you back, I've got some dickhead next to me answering all my questions"

COOPERISMS!

My friend drowned in a bowl of muesli. A strong currant pulled him in.

A guy walks into the psychiatrist wearing only
Clingfilm for shorts. The shrink says, "Well, I can clearly
see you're nuts."

A man came round in hospital after a serious accident.
He shouted, "Doctor, doctor, I can't feel my legs!"
The doctor replied, "I know you can't, I've cut your
arms off".

Man goes to the doctor, with a strawberry growing out of his head.
Doc says "I'd better give you some cream to put on that."

A man takes his Rottweiler to the vet.
    "My dog's cross-eyed, is there anything you can do for him?"
    "Well," says the vet, "let's have a look at him"
    So he picks the dog up and examines his eyes, then checks his teeth.

Finally, he says,
    "I'm going to have to put him down."
    "What? Because he's cross-eyed?"
    "No, because he's really heavy"

Police arrested two kids yesterday, one was drinking battery acid, the other
was eating fireworks.

They charged one and let the other one off.

Breaststroke Rules?

There was a competition to cross the English Channel doing only the
breaststroke, and the three women who entered the race were a brunette, a redhead and a blonde.
After approximately 14 hours, the brunette staggered up on the shore and was declared the fastest breaststroker.
About 40 minutes later, the redhead crawled up on the shore and was declared the second place finisher.
Nearly 4 hours after that, the blonde finally came ashore and promptly collapsed in front of the worried onlookers.
When the reporters asked why it took her so long to complete the race, she replied, "I don't want to sound like I'm a sore loser, but I think those two other girls were using their arms..."

Did She Say Anything?

His wife had been killed in an accident and the police were questioning Finnegan. "Did she say anything before she died?" asked the sergeant.
"Well yes, yes she did...
She spoke without interruption for about forty years," said the Finnegan.

<u>Subject: Two Drunken Women.........</u>

Two women friends, incredibly drunk and walking home got caught short.

They were very near a graveyard and one of them suggested they do their business behind a head stone or something. One of them had nothing to wipe with so she thought she'd take off her panties and use them, then throw them away. Her friend however was wearing a rather expensive underwear set and didn't want to ruin hers but was lucky enough to salvage a large ribbon from a wreath that was on one of the graves and proceeded to wipe herself with that. They then made off for home.

The next day one woman's husband phoned the other husband and said "We'd better keep an eye on our wives you know, mine came home last night without her panties."

"That's nothing" said the other "Mine came back with a card stuck between her ass that said 'From all the lads at the fire station. We'll never forget you'."

Smile – it's the second best thing you can do with your lips

Please Don't Let Me Be Misunderstood

The Queen was visiting one of London's top hospitals and she specified she wanted to see absolutely everything.

During her tour of the floors she passed a room where a male patient
was w*nking.
"Oh my", said the Queen, "that's disgraceful, what is the meaning of this?"

The Consultant leading the tour explains; "I am sorry Ma'am, but this man has a very serious medical condition and is only following doctors orders. His body produces too much semen and his testicles keep overfilling. Until we can find out exactly what is causing this problem he's been instructed to do that at least 5 times a day or there is a danger that his testicles will explode, and he would die instantly."

"Oh, I am so sorry", said the Queen, "I totally misunderstood the situation".

On the next floor they passed a room where a young nurse was giving a patient a blow-job.
"Oh how disgusting", said the Queen, "What's happening in there?"

The Doctor replied,
"Same problem, but he's got BUPA cover."

Subject: Inner peace

I am passing this on to you because it was passed on to me and has
definitely worked for me. By following the simple advice I read
in an article, I have finally found inner peace........

It reads: "The way to achieve inner peace is to finish all the
things you've started."
So I looked around to see all the things I had started and
hadn't finished.
So, today I have finished one bottle of vodka, a bottle of red
wine, a bottle of Jack Daniel's, my Prozac, a small box of chocolates
and a case of Heineken.....You have no idea how good I feel!!!
Pass this on to those you feel are in need of Inner Peace.

~~~~~~~~~~~~~~~~~~~~~~~~~~~~~~~~~

Yet Another Essex Girl Story

A woman goes to the doctor's office. "Doctor, I've got a strange
problem that I need your opinion on.", "Could you describe the
symptoms to me?" he asked. "Well, it's easier if I show you," she said
and standing up, proceeded to undress. When she was down to her
underwear she sat on the edge of the examining table and spread
her legs to reveal two small green circles on her inner thighs. "They
don't hurt or anything, but I was a little worried about them." The
doctor peered closely at the two circles and said, "Are you a lesbian,
by any chance?" he asked. Embarrassed and slightly non-plussed at
this question coming from a man with his head between her thighs
she replied "Well, yes, I am actually. Why do you ask?",
"Well, I'm afraid you'll have to tell your girlfriend that her earrings
aren't real gold."

How to get your kids to do better in Maths!

Little Zachary, a Jewish kid, was doing very badly in maths. His parents had tried everything: tutors, mentors, flash cards, special learning centres, in short, everything they could think of to help his maths.

Finally, in a last ditch effort, they took Zachary down and enrolled him in the local Catholic school.

After the first day, little Zachary came home with a very serious look on his face. He didn't even kiss his mother hello.

Instead, he went straight to his room and started studying. Books and papers were spread out all over the room and little Zachary was hard at work. His mother was amazed. She called him down to dinner and, to her shock, the minute he was done he marched back to his room without a word and, in no time, he was back hitting the books as hard as before.

This went on for some time, day after day while the mother tried to understand what made all the difference. Finally, little Zachary brought home his school report. He quietly laid it on the table, went up to his room, and hit the books.

With great trepidation, his Mum looked at it and, to her great surprise, little Zachary got an "A" in maths. She could no longer hold her curiosity.

She went to his room and said: "Fantastic Son! So what was it? Was it the nuns?"

Little Zachary looked at her and shook his head. "No," he whispered.

"Well, then," she replied, "was it the books, the discipline, the structure, the uniforms? WHAT was it?"

Little Zachary looked at her and said: "Well, on the first day of school, when I saw that guy nailed to the plus sign, I knew they weren't fucking around."

And finally, remember...

**Be nice to your kids;
they'll choose your
nursing home!**

Can **you** do better?

A collection of stories like these takes a long time to put together and there will always be people that know lots of better jokes and stories than these and will never be able to publish them.

Well, now you can!!

The PPGS publishing team is already well into the next collection and if you would like to submit a joke for book 3, and we publish it, we will give you a credit and send you a free copy of the next book.

Please send your joke or story, in writing to:

PPGS, PO Box 42, Princes Risborough, Bucks. HP27 0XH

If you would like to be informed when the next book is due out and perhaps have a copy reserved, please write to the address above or email to info@ppgs.co.uk

We still have a few copies of Book 1 available – if you have missed it and would like one sent to you, just write or email us and we will send you a copy whilst stocks l